Advance Praise for *Transitions*

Reading this wonderful book gave me utmost enjoyment. It is multi-layered and ever so magical, containing personal and national facets in a rich harmony of sharp contrasts – a harmony that combines the complexity of the mind with the wisdom of the heart.

I was deeply moved by the humaneness of your writing, by the sincerity and softness expressed mostly in the second person, by the power of your insatiable creativity, which knows no limits and never ceases to excite, inspire and intrigue. Mostly, however, this is an autobiography of highly courageous acts and inspiring ideas.

-Shimon Peres, Former President of Israel

The sad chapters are heartbreaking without being sentimental; the death of [her] brother Assi is shattering, as are the complex feelings toward [her] father [Moshe Dayan]. And yet, sickness and death, pain and old age do not make this a depressing book -- they are overcome by love and an unquenchable thirst for life ...love of children and grandchildren, of books and poetry, pursuing a rational and moral political line. I admired what the book lacks -- bitterness and resentment – [for] it is written throughout in a spirit that is bold, courageous and lucid.

-Amos Oz

A brave book by a brave woman. It describes, with honesty, with crystal accuracy and talent, a life experience that is both exhilarating and painful.

-Etgar Keret

In a precise, rich and candid language, Yael Dayan wanders through her dramatic life with captivating courage and honesty.

-Abraham B. Yehoshua

Here we find that rare miracle, when a life becomes literature, and in this case it is great literature.

-Dr. Giddon Ticotsky

D1595871

Yael Dayan's lovely memoir looks death in the eye with impressive honesty…What makes it interesting is that Dayan is not reconciled to her status as a pensioner… She describes the process of dying with impressive, and sometimes stirring, honesty…Her beautiful, poetic monologue expresses the heart-felt groans of old-time Israelis.

-Ofri Ilany, *Yedioth Ahronoth,*

She touches on things without embellishing, and also without trepidation … Transitions gives us the sober observation of her own life by someone who has reached the fullness of years…and also on Israeli society and the changes it has undergone since its inception. And within all of this, there is much beauty.

-Author Ilan Sheinfeld,

Yael Dayan has not lost one gram of her courage and determination. … I read her lovely book in a storm of emotion. Sadness, regret and compassion swirled and switched among the lines.

-Dina Haluts, La'Isha,

Yael Dayan tells her story frankly…Despite the difficulties, the disappointments, there is a fine thread of optimism in the book.

-Ora Armoni, Kol Israel

Transitions
A Memoir

Library and Archives Canada Cataloguing in Publication
Dayan, Yael, 1939-
[Minegged. English]
      Transitions / Yael Dayan.

Includes bibliographical references and index.
Issued in print and electronic formats.
ISBN 978-1-77161-207-4 (paperback).--ISBN 978-1-77161-208-1
(html).--ISBN 978-1-77161-209-8 (pdf)
 1. Dayan, Yael, 1939-. 2. Political activists--Israel--
Biography. 3. Politicians--Israel--Biography. 4. Pacifists--Israel--
Biography. 5. Authors--Israel--Biography. 6. Israel--Biography.

      I. Title. II. Title: Minegged. English

DS126.6.D29A3 2016   956.9405092   C2016-904348-7
                                                 C2016-904349-5

Published by Mosaic Press, Oakville, Ontario, Canada, 2016.
Copyright © 2016 Yael Dayan
Translation Copyright © 2016 Yael Dayan
Cover photograph by Gal Hermoni, © 2016 Gal Hermoni / La'Isha Magazine
Printed and bounded in Canada
Designed by Courtney Blok
Published by arrangement with the Institute of the Translation of Hebrew Literature (ITHL).
Supported by: "Am Ha-Sefer" – The Israeli Fund for Translation of Hebrew Books.

The Cultural Administration, Israel Ministry of Culture and Sport

We acknowledge the Ontario Arts Council
for their support of our publishing program
We acknowledge the Ontario Media Development Corporation
for their support of our publishing program

Transitions
A Memoir

Yael Dayan

Translated by Maya Klein

Other Works by Yeal Dayan:

Non-Fiction:

Israel Journal: June, 1967 [Also known as *A Soldier's Diary*] (1967)

My Father, His Daughter (1985)

Novels:

New Face in the Mirror (1959)

Envy the Frightened (1961)

Dust (1963)

Death Had Two Sons (1967)

Three Weeks in October (1979)

For Alma, Yasmin, Adam, Boaz
my grandchildren, my life.

In every waiting for, a never,
the sadness of Nevo.

-Ra'hel

Preface

A memoir is not an autobiography. The way I see it, my memoir is committed to the truth and to nothing but the truth; but not to all the truth.

Transitions is not a biography written in chronological order. The choices I made prioritize topics, public and personal, using subjective criteria that may seem random. However, they reflect their importance in particular chapters of my life. Thus, great loves, tragic losses, flora and fauna, trivial daily affairs and national wars-of survival or of choice-are tossed in with what appears to be the same cerebral or emotional importance.

I took the liberty of writing about my own transitions: from the naïve Israeli teen-ager and soldier to the sophisticated and indulged best-selling writer; and from there all the way to the mature, wise old woman, looking back with a degree of frustration on dreams never to be fulfilled.

And I also write about the transitions I endured and experienced pertaining to the State of Israel: from a beloved, admired, victorious and just homeland, via an unbearable regression, to the dangerous sphere of ethno-theocratic messianic existence, which is so far-removed from a peace- and justice-seeking society. The Israel that has become occupier of the Palestinian people's land and rights, in the name of God's promise and the false alibi of Security.

Transitions moves across continents and eras, through past, present and future, and deals with both the public and the intimate. Written with love, pain, freedom and an honest longing to share, it is not devoid of hope for a better future.

Perhaps loneliness is what caused the frequent switches between the first-person narrator to the voice of the second-person. In addition to myself, "I", recounting and telling, there is also another me, observing, witnessing, daring to search deeper and addressing myself as "you", conversing intimately with me.

Yes, I am telling the reader a story, but I am also talking to myself with you, the reader, listening in.

Chapter 1

At 74, longing for myself as I was. As a young attractive soldier in the Israeli Army? As a best-selling "jet-set" young writer? Daughter of legendary one-eyed General Moshe Dayan? The bride of Colonel Dov Sion who I met in the battlefield of the Six Day War? Mother of two, The Peace activist *Knesset* Deputy? Longing or accepting the here and now?

You can sense the pitiful gap between what you want and what you are able to do. To achieve, give or receive. You know that this gap is not merely rooted in the self-evident– the biological clock, the betrayal of the body, the weakening eyesight, the weariness in the hips and knees, but rather in something deeper. You rigorously examine the gap for you are alone. You have no one with you to express your self-pity in words or in physical contact.

The purpose of living, the will to carry on as opposed to the readiness to die, the fatigue that accompanies despair. You don't have a witness; a reliable witness to your life, your crises, the gentle fluctuations of feelings of satisfaction and disappointment, There will also be no witness to your desire to go on or to end it. A mirror, like paper, is not a witness. Shatter it if you wish, or change and improve it, shorten, extend. You try not to want what you cannot have, not to think of your outstretched hand that is too short to reach the light, try not to yearn for the witness who is no longer here, the love that has floated to a far-off, unintelligible place.

Longing? You long for yourself as you used to be. The way that you think you were. The way you wanted to be?

The way you were when? At seventeen and a half? In your army uniform? Your skin smooth, perpetually tan, your long hair cascading, a twinkle in your hazel eyes, a flirtatious smile playing on your lips, curious and brave, without commitment, without loyalty, dangerously and recklessly self-confident, aware of your attractiveness, intriguing, a girl-woman who doesn't know what she wants or where she wants to go.
The way you were as a young writer? In the world's drawing rooms and literary salons, in the gossip columns and on the pages of the book reviews. With a good figure, tastefully, expensively dressed. Make-up free, toying with your suitors, skipping across continents, cities, languages, publishers, launches, galas, your first novel, second, third.

Yael Dayan

My curiosity knew no bounds. I felt that there was an entire world waiting for my footsteps, a world beyond Europe and North America. Different cultures, languages, landscapes, flora and colors ripe with secrets and rhythms unknown to me. A world that was not a few hours away by airplane– but would be revealed in a gradual, reassuring journey that prepares one for the transition between continents and cultures and makes the discovery richer and more surprising. I took up a publisher's offer to go to Brazil and another publisher's invitation to Argentina and set out for a continent new to me, traveling, as I loved it, by way of sea.

Your longest and most wonderful sail was from Haifa to Brazil on a ZIM cargo ship. You set off with books and travel guides and a stack of blank paper for your third novel. You were introduced to the power of the isolating ocean that can shift without warning– gently swaying or stormily tossing you about. After close to a week of thrilling and rough sailing, when you crossed the equator to the southern hemisphere, the crew doused you with a pail of water, as is customary for sailors celebrating their "first time" and from then on the North Star disappeared from the sky and was replaced by the Southern Cross.

It was as if the long voyage had cut the umbilical cord and when you reached Brazil, your sense of time was severed from that of home. It was a different way of counting, separating the world into what lies between the tropic of Cancer and the tropic of Capricorn, the habitat you are comfortable with, and what lies beyond them to the north and the south, the balmy regions where the sun is never at its zenith, and onwards to the north and south where the circles gradually narrow into ice and cold.

You travelled far from home but you remained addicted to it. Your frequent, but brief visits home failed to form close friendships, caused your relationship with your family to flatten and become superficial, and threatened the deep roots of your love for your country.

The rift widened between you and your home, your family, country, language– and the new world, the languages you acquired, the knowledge that was accumulating, the curiosity that was being quenched, the soft landings and the easy escapes, the seemingly safe anchors and the true friendships, and you began to ask yourself questions of identity. Jewish, Israeli, cosmopolitan, Middle-Eastern, citizen of the Western world? Questions posed by quick success and a misleading sense of freedom of choice.

Do you long for the way you were as a mother? With the maturity and calm of someone having returned from a long journey, your bag bursting with abundance, from the baby's cradle to the kindergarten lunchbox, the school bag, the son's and daughter's army uniforms, meatballs and schnitzel, mashed potatoes and rice, graduation ceremonies, good health, ripeness.

Curbing the imagination and subjecting it to documentation in the last book you wrote after your father's death.[1] Anxious concern for your children, the expectations you never expressed, your hopes for their futures. At home, overseeing its manage-

---

1 Yael Dayan, *My Father, His Daughter*, 1985.

ment and also working from it as long as the children weren't independent and Dov's time was not his own. Full, rich years that manifested everything you thought a home and a family should be.

The way you were as a combatant member of parliament? A revolutionary, ardent feminist trying to change the old, established norms, ruthless in the defense of human rights, clashing with the dogmatic Judaic halacha, occasionally succeeding in opening a new path with like-minded allies, admired, hated, envied, ambitious and intolerant of deception and ignorance, of superficiality, a friend to the needy and downtrodden and less so to colleagues when teamwork was required. Not fully aware of the need to compromise.

What do you miss, what kind of happiness is now out of reach? Is it a longing for the self-satisfaction that came with your public roles? For the focus and determination required for achieving concrete results? To be accessible to the public, the paths to the hearts of voters, the attempt to remove the stumbling blocks of discrimination, ignorance and darkness.

Or perhaps simply the regular day-to-day experience, an occasional touch of passion, an embrace, the attention, interest and desire to do things together. Not to fear honesty, or be afraid of expressing and accepting criticism, not to walk on eggshells, be self-righteous and defensive, not to hide. To love and be loved.

When did the balance between the lust for life and the preoccupation with death shift? When did good health give way to illness and pain, both temporary and chronic, of you and those close to you? When was the confidence in changing the odds, in remedies, in the triumph of the spirit and the struggle, exchanged for the compassion enfolding the end and the belief in your ability to soften it?

Did it happen a decade ago, when Dov's incurable illness took a turn for the worse and the long years of parting from him ended, or did it take place with the twisted life and death of Dahlia? [2] When the cancer in your body was discovered, or with the diagnosis of the disease that has been constricting your lungs? The short life of your father? The wondrous old age of your mother? When did the broad, all-encompassing, forward facing gaze grow dim and give way to a frightened counting of last lines and brief glimpses of the remains?

And perhaps the balance was only recently upset, in the present, when you fell and were injured, fracturing your back, your hip and a fair share of your spirit. You could not restrain the pain and could not remember how you fell and thus you sensed that death too could pay you an unexpected visit. Just as its signs had crept toward Aharona, without warning.

And now the pain tears you apart. Piercing and catching in the pelvis and never subsiding, it flows like an electrical current from your hip down to your thigh and pounds at your kneecap and you don't stifle the cry-shout-scream-moan-wail, and you fall from the realm of thought to the bottom of the pathetic, shameful, wretched

---

2 Dahlia Ravikovitch (1936-2005) an Israeli poet, author of some twenty volumes and one of the most prominent and distinctive voices in contemporary Hebrew poetry. Herein will be referred to as "Dahlia."

barrel. You want to sit down. A small and unattainable desire. To be able to sit without pain. You sat and watched your sister-in-law Aharona flicker out, she had grown tired of her life decades ago but could not go through with the act of ending it, and at the end of her life, when the sentence had already been given and was about to be carried out, she clung to the slow dripping of the wax pooling on the end of the candle.

You did not know her well. Not what was hidden from the eye. A beautiful woman, ten years younger than you. You felt responsibility and tender affection for her children. Your paths crossed in the beauty of a "double wedding," your marriages took place on the same night, you were a radiant bride who had just returned from the wide world to the sand dunes of the Sinai Desert, to war and love, and she was overflowing with youthful beauty as she took her place beside your younger brother, the handsome prince. And the years passed and the two couples grew distant, the courses of their lives separated.

After she divorced your brother, you loved her from afar but were a life- saver in times of crisis, always there to lend a hand before returning to your other, separate path.

You sit with her every day, despite your own pain and hardship, you sit next to her, by the side of her bed and at its head. You bend over the face that framed her former beauty and she opens her eyes– perhaps in recognition – and then closes them again in resignation. And in the intensity, the awkwardness and silence that the proximity of death entails, you imagine your own death. For a moment you want to trade places with her, to be swallowed up by the thick blanket, with only your face and hands showing, examining the soft parting from life, "hovering at a low altitude," toes touching the ground and head floating elsewhere– eyes closed and jaw slack and you become aware of your voice again, open your eyes willingly, reacting, murmuring, giving a smile of surrender.

And so it goes day after day, with the evenings filled with the coming and going of visitors. Discussing her tranquility, her lack of suffering, the way she opened her eyes, or closed them, about her pulse, thirst, dryness and how beautiful and loved she is– the most beautiful and admired woman.

Of all the things that were uttered, you chose what was of most interest to you: to die at home, painlessly and without suffering, fewer people, fewer attempts to revive memories. Without the childish tones. A person who is dying and in the throes of a metastasized brain is no longer a child and will not comprehend baby talk. You wouldn't want to prolong the twilight time and encounter the impatience of those waiting for the inevitable and irrevocable.

The doctor told you that round-the-clock, quality care prolongs life. "By how long?" you asked, a day or two. And two days passed and then another two.

These were the doctor's orders: no oxygen, no drink, no food. But it is impossible to leave a thirsty person without water or a breathless one without oxygen, and the prolongation of the days and the hours that is accompanied by a smile, deceptive as it is, still allows for a sense of confidence in our power over nature and medical prognoses. Perhaps a sudden, quick death is better, you mused as Aharona lay at her deathbed for weeks, as the sharp pain of mourning and the *shiva* had already taken place every day for the duration of her final days, and her obituary had already been prepared, and everything was known in advance– there would be a final burst of tears when the funeral service finally took place, and the days of the shiva would be shortened and deliveries would arrive from the catering company with food that would be too sweet or too salty.

Evening. Death tarries and her chest rises and falls in the laborious act of breathing, her mouth sucks water from a straw, there is no urine, no food, there is just a fading ember of life and a group of people watching the body in its decline, and no– you don't want a sudden, ugly death– not the crushing of limbs, or the remnants of an accident, not organ failure unconscious in a hospital.

If you could choose a death, why not make it come quicker, choose the timing, be in bed, a beautiful woman with a bright face, opening and closing her eyes and soaking up the words, the eulogies, the list of virtues, smiling with the look of one who is gathering colorful glass beads which have no use, in life or death. And among the cheap glass who would spot a diamond or an emerald. You have to keep the real spark, retain it, nurture it, remember it. That is the mark that you want to leave. You think about the written mark that you want to leave behind. Not a will, but an explanation, because the patience of those close to you is wearing thin.

> "What gets left of a man amounts to a part. To his
> spoken part. To a part of speech." [3]

You wanted to write your spoken part.

And during the final moments you were at her side with her children, her hand in yours, you felt the remainder of life draining out– the pulse weakening and disappearing, the final flutter of the vein in the neck, the cold cheek and the unresponsive hand, the open eyes fixed until her daughter gently closes them, forever. A slight twitch in the corner of the mouth facing me, body fluids leaking, pooling in a wrinkle and you wipe them away.

Silence. A murmur of agreement that this is the end, eyes that do not meet. You let go of the hand and the pulse which your fingers were gripping as if you could squeeze out one more beat, and you left the room.

The threads of love and tenderness that were woven in the days and nights of anticipation began to unravel with the finality of death. The acceptance that preceded death hovered gently like a shroud ready and waiting to wrap and return to the dust, and most of the tears were shed before the hour of death.

To return to dust in a box, a plain wood coffin in a small friendly cemetery with flowers to soften the knock of the wet earth against the coffin, like an elaborate layer

---

3 Joseph Brodsky, "A Part of Speech."

cake. The freesias and the anemones, and after them the red earth of the orange groves that once grew there, and then another layer of flowers and a damp mound covered with a fragrant floral carpet and a sign–where the head rests–and in the future a tombstone.

As you expected, the shiva, which had actually begun when it became clear that there was no hope, seemed redundant and was shortened to include the people who had eulogized Aharona while she was alive and her death refused to come. The obituaries, the final arrangements, selling her apartment and dividing the valuables between her children and friends, and the trips that her grieving children took and always seemed hasty– east to Thailand and west to New York. The remains of the stitches that unraveled were left in your hands, webs that asked for comfort and consolation between the memory and nothingness.

How fragile, how fleeting was the familial fabric, the network that salvages from the eternal nature of death or the transience of life, suspended over nothing. How little is left.

Three days after Aharona's funeral, when the mourning, the memory and the questioning had all evaporated like the trail of a jet in the distance, I went in for more surgery and then the East heat wave began. The pain returned, pounding like a sledgehammer, alleviated with frustrating slowness by medication and my stubborn progression with the pain, against the pain, until it finally improved. And when it improved I remained seated, surrounded by emptiness.

I am trying to put a date to the beginning of the fall, my fall, which began absentmindedly. The ground that slipped away under my feet, or perhaps the rock that cracked wide open. When was I disrupted? The question never ceases to plague me.

At first there were the dreams– moving from tranquil to threatening ones, sweat drenched nights when only wide open eyes could ward off the demons. My father and Dov disappeared from my dreams in a flash, as if I had come within burning distance of them and they were pleasant in their warmth– the routine of climbing of a tree, a lover's walk, playing hopscotch as father calls me to come inside, Dov and I in uniform, exchanging words and loving in between lines– it never returned. When did I become depleted, and not with a single blow that severed limbs or layers.

Then, about three years after Dov's death, your female body disappears. You no longer touch a soft thigh or embrace yourself taking pleasure in the flesh and the smooth, rounded skin.

You no longer wake up wet without knowing if you were indulging in fantasy or in an act of love with the familiar and beloved.

During the long years of Dov's illness you almost succumbed to the temptation of a stranger and twice, before you were married, you had lengthy and complicated relations in hidden corners and drank stolen water that was sweeter than honey and left you desiring more. You preserved your beauty, your supple curves, enticing wit and the generosity that contained everything a lover could want. You were careful not to provoke, not to attempt to transcend– as in the days when you were free and dripping with the nectar of youth– the feminine maturity and intelligent proportion of a courted woman.

Now you remember the feeling but do not revive it. You do not touch yourself or take those paths that soar to the peaks and gently bring you down enveloped in calm and comfort. You tell yourself the stories, reconstruct the facts, name the cities, the hotel rooms and the items, counting the lover's gifts and recounting the crossing of continents to meet in clandestine places. You force yourself to remember every detail, reinforcing the sharpness of your mind. You regret destroying the letters, hundreds of lovers' letters, letters of love, not insinuated but explicit, adorned with poetry, express- ing a thirst and a hunger for what you apparently gave freely, generously, both in body and spirit. Letters betraying names and titles and countries that you were afraid would fall into the wrong hands and reveal the great passions, the soaring romances and the ones that faded elegantly with mutual respect. You erased the signs and the omens and kept the stories in your mind and blood and not in your nerve ends.

You also kept the disappointments and stories of abandonment– by you and of you.

And when the margins of memory began to fade, after Dahlia's death, you dug through your papers to look for signs and remnants, lest a stranger not believe you when you told the tangled tales of these loves and they would be wiped away without a trace. The body still desired and you felt a slight tremor pass through you at the oc- casions intended for love. Alone on a stormy night, when the thunder closes in on you and the lightning ignites desire; or in the crushing heat of afternoon as you lie naked on the big bed with the shades drawn and the silence crawls over every cell of your skin and each curve awakens the wisp of a memory of a soft, barely discernable caress.

And that too is over. You turn into a book-keeper afraid of forgetting those in- debted to you and make do with jotting down abbreviations of names and places, the fear of losing your memory is stronger than the wish to revive emotions and the body ceases to give and take pleasure. Sometimes, when you are courted– with a light touch or a telling look–you grow fearful, because you no longer love yourself. You avoid the mirror, do not meet your reflection, crumple close-up photos and examine the backs of your hands with unforgiving pity–the brown age spots and bulging veins like pipes twisted in the blazing heat. You cover yourself from your own eyes so as not to see the breast that underwent surgery, disfigured as if it had been bitten into, twice, by a voracious animal rather than the careful knife of the surgeon who had removed the lethal growths.

You no longer wear tank-tops or sleeveless shirts because your arms seem as loose as a double chin. How unfortunate that the short, casual young fashion no longer suits you. You long for a different century that you had never wanted to live in– with ruffles and lace, high collars and slimming corsets, long velvet dresses in shades of ol- ive green, clothes that dress old age in dignified gowns, or caressing chemises and silk nightgowns. The same nightgowns that you have in your closet, ones that still flatter your slim shoulders and smooth legs.

After bathing, you moisturize the dry wrinkled skin of your arms, the prominent blue veins, your face, forehead and cheeks thirstily absorb the moisture and the light flowery fragrance. You do not fool yourself that the wrinkles will disappear. But grooming is important to you, in itself.

Are you beautiful? You were beautiful. You cannot pinpoint the year that it changed, the moment it shifted. You can spot the decline, the worry lines, the thinning of the hair and the eyebrows after you underwent radiation, but you also see what remains. The shining, intelligent eyes, the high cheekbones that stretch the skin around the eyes and at the hollow of the cheeks, the features that haven't changed. When did you become a reminder of what you once were, a public figure, recognized on the street and at social events but with a brief moment of hesitation before the connection is made between what people remember and what they see. "Excuse me, you look like…" people say to you.

"You remind me of…" and you confirm reluctantly, with false modesty, "Yes, it's me, I mean– it is me," and try to locate the moment, the year, the tolling of the bell that announced the wrinkling, the drying up, the marks of time. And something beyond that too. The aging personality, the erosion of energy, lethargic remainders replacing what once were sensitive nerve ends, outstretched extremities that reached out curiously in every direction have become accumulations of cells folded inwards, turned in on themselves.

I am drawing a ladder and trying to scale everything that happened from rung to rung. A flexible ladder, a kind of diagram that soars and descends, rises and flattens out, and I try to see where the missing rungs are, to map out the upsurges and the crushing falls. Trying to signpost my life.

Memory lapse? Repression? Selectivity? Grey cells that have degenerated and turned the tables, made the essential redundant and pushed the marginal to the center. Instead of a delicate feather pen, sorting and inscribing, I manage to identify the coarse strokes of a broad paintbrush.

It could have happened this way or another and I attempt to determine the milestones in the decades that have passed, fighting forgetfulness and lining it with memories– are they real? fabricated? What's the difference between imagination and memory if both are in my mind? Without witnesses, without a record, in any case the only definite things are the starting and ending points. Most of my life is now behind me, that is certain, and in the years remaining there are few specks of light and they too flicker between the tangible and the illusory. Personal fantasies have been packed up and set aside. I cling desperately to what I cannot abandon. The goals without which life– the one lived and the one left to endure– is unworthy.

I try to delineate periods of time and mark them with milestones. Whatever amnesia left untouched and what has not been shut away in the closed room that is bolted from within. I find it easier to scale my journey with threads of emotion–longing, regret, desire and disappointment. To wander with a sure step and visit the places I once inhabited, thus gaining a better understanding of the hesitation and fear when I confront what awaits me, crawling along the last mile, faded and dizzy with fatigue.

Chapter 2

2011.At 72 moving to a new apartment in Tel Aviv. Jasmine and Falcons and same the locked room.

The packers arrived to finish filling the boxes. The movers, who came after them, weren't sure that the crane could withstand the wind on the stormy day I left the apartment where Dov and I had lived for over a decade. If not for Dov's illness and his decline into a loneliness aligned with my own, I would never have moved. I wouldn't have looked for and found an apartment that faced a different direction, was on a different floor, and paved with terracotta tiles. With his death, like someone bypassing the source of searing sadness, I left behind everything I could part with and only took whatever resisted removal, ligatures of disaster and slivers of radiance.

Without pain or regret I let go of the home of his illness and suffering, passing it on to the new owners to be demolished and renovated as they saw fit.

I left behind the years of commuting to Jerusalem, to the Knesset, the Israeli Parliament, the election years, successes and failures and began to adjust to other patterns, diminishing in both the public eye as well as my own. It wasn't a complete disappearance but an existence that wit-hdrew to the second and third tiers of activity and recognition of my capabilities; as admiring embraces and accolades dwindled and were replaced–I felt–by disdain, contempt, dismissal and even oblivion. The apartment that I left behind was too large, rather run down, its flaws were hidden beneath the carpets and the paintings on the walls. There was a massive library that I had weeded out over the years, but still included many superfluous items. Books which would never be read again, encyclopedias that had been replaced by computer programs, victory albums and obsolete war albums, outdated lexicons missing decades of progress, thought and creativity.

In the apartment that I sold there was also a locked room.

Your face reddens and your hand hesitates as you write the words locked room. In it, you imprisoned everything you wanted to erase and repress, and the contents crawl like molten lava, seeking an outlet and stopping at the wall of your shame. You do not want to delete it and you cannot forget, only hide from strangers. Every so often you enter the room, like someone who knows a secret code. You thumb through the letters that remained after you destroyed many of them, you look at forbidden pictures and reconstruct the failures, the harsh words flung at you, the slack and irreparable line tying you to your children and the insults and affronts. Your wrinkled skin absorbs the silk of the former passions, the secret joys in numbered rooms and in cities that were not stamped in your passport.

In the locked room the files are arranged according to the emotional intensity of the words, according to the actions taken and the ones avoided and the various periods of your life– not in chronological order but according to the various points of view– internal, external, long-term relations, relations that were severed– you as a mother, you and the wars, your shame and disgrace, your abusers.

You and your lovers and loves and you–on your own. In the past two decades–on your own.

You've been living in your new apartment for more than a year , the locked room was not left behind in the big dark apartment. It migrated with you, changed its storage space. Now it resides in boxes and drawers and safes and in enigmatic cobwebs that only you can discern.

Before I sold the apartment, I had a big argument with my children and friends. "Under no circumstances should you sell, you won't find anything else suitable, you won't have a place to live and you'll run out of money, you won't be able to handle the renovations, you don't have it in you now because you're unwell and haven't got the energy." I felt that the resentment and criticism stemmed from their fear that this little "adventure" of mine, as they called it, would eventually become a burden on them.

Nonetheless, I sold the apartment, made ample time to find another, a different place, suitable for me– just for me, and for the concluding chapter of what seemed to me the short period remaining for the rest of my life.

And when I found it, I could picture exactly how I wanted it taken apart and rebuilt, the architect would advise, but I'd be in charge, as usual. I would keep some of the furniture and design the space to accommodate the artwork that I love, my brother Udi's sculptures, the slimmed down library, each volume carefully selected, a dining table for family dinners, and my desk, the same one I have been using for over four decades, which has migrated with me from one apartment to another. I reupholstered the sofa with the rounded edges, which I bought with the old apartment and it changed its skin– from the dark pink velvet I purchased at a Cairo fabric shop to coffee-colored leather. I sorted out the kitchenware and packed up a box of polished silverware to be stored. The oriental rugs were rolled up and packed away, a carpet from Tehran, gifts from the Shah, carpets from bazaars all over the world– bought, exchanged, ones which had covered large expanses of the old apartment. Not all of them could be accommodated and I needed to feel lighter, shedding layers of bourgeoisie heirlooms, obsolete memorabilia, dust-gathering objects whose origin I could not even be sure of. Almost younger.

I moved into the new apartment with my belongings and the old Armenian ceramic sign bearing our names on the front door– mine and Dov's– just as before, only with a different feeling. Stripped of a degree of sensitivity, of illusions and expectations of myself, and a little less vulnerable to criticism from those close to me, without loving them less.

Not exactly healthy, supporting myself with a cane, my hips aching, suffering from chronic lung insufficiency but nonetheless, I still had a sense of a new beginning.

I moved into the new apartment missing the birds and plants that were such an important part of my life in the big apartment by the sea. In the old apartment, the plants thrived in expansive window boxes, enchanting with their scents of jasmine and stephanotis and with the vibrant colors of the blooming creepers– the ones that could survive the salty western breeze. They shielded the ground floor apartment from the street, cloaking it in a green expanse which blocked both light and air. There were problems with the plants on the west side of the new apartment. The bougainvillea didn't bloom, and only a single creeping rose had survived of the many I planted; it climbed the grating, pale and scraggly.

A hollyhock, a tiny seedling that was a gift from my friend Orly, flourished, grew and towered to two meters height, its huge pink blossoms overflowing from their flowerpot to the great delight of my granddaughters, who liked repeating the name "hollyhock." My granddaughters and I took a potted plant which did not need sunlight and transformed it into a "dessert-tree" inspired by a well-loved children's book. The tree boasted lollipops and marshmallows, chocolate and fruit flavored toffee, which after a meal the girls could "pick" from the dessert-tree, to their parents' displeasure and the awe of their friends, reinforcing their pride in their grandmother's uniqueness.

In the window box in the grand-children's room–they were only granddaughters until their brother was born– each little girl had her own seasonal flowers which bloomed in joyful colors and bulbs which sprouted– with a fair degree of success– into hyacinths and narcissi.

And there were the birds. In our first apartment as a family, before we moved to the apartment by the sea, there was a falcon's nest. The falcons were permanent residents on our kitchen porch. They arrived by chance and stayed as a result of my efforts. First I watched them, then I placed a small cut of raw meat on the windowsill and the porch.

The falcons pounced on the meat and hovered nearby, expecting a second course, and then noticed me placing the offering and disappearing into the house.

They returned time after time, coming to snatch the meat and sometimes even eating on the porch before flying off. Once they got used to me, I put on a thick kitchen glove and held the meat in my hand and much to my surprise, they weren't deterred by my presence and oftentimes ate from my hand or from the windowsill. I changed the menu– raw chicken necks sliced in two, which they could dig their claws into more easily. I kept a large amount in my freezer, which was well-stocked with falcon-food, to the butcher's bewilderment, who had no clue that the copious amounts of chicken-necks I was buying actually served to feed wild birds of prey.

Dov joined the adventure and regarded it as a natural occurrence that a farm girl like me should adopt a pair of falcons. The wild birds became part of the family. The children watched them courting and building their nest on the porch, laying their spotted eggs, taking care of them– the food dropped from my hands into the nest regularly, and when the goslings hatched I improved the quality of the meat, as befitting babies. After one or two nesting seasons, curious people began dropping by in order to observe the adopted family. Ornithologists and bird lovers came to our house to watch the couple and their goslings, already mature and able to fly– as they would take off in flight and glide at a precise distance, and then, as accurately as a cruise missile, swiftly swoop down and slow to land on the chicken neck that rested on the railing or lay flat in the palm of my hand.

When we moved to the big apartment by the sea, we said goodbye to the falcons and I moved from the spectacular, the rare and the lofty, to the common birds of the house and backyard. I tempted them on a regular basis and they arrived in droves to eat the seeds, landing from the roof or coming from the ground, to the exclamations of the children and the delight of the grandchildren.

I became like my grandmother Dvora from Nahalal, who would scatter seeds and cluck her tongue at the chickens around her. The wild pigeons populated a high voltage wire opposite my windows that faced the street. Following a brief period of mistrust and hesitation, they began pecking at the slices of bread that I placed on the windowsills.

After a while I improved the offering and bought bags of bird seed– and in time sacks of it– which I presented to them twice a day, in large clay plates placed strategically in the yard. The number of birds increased from a few to dozens to over a hundred wild pigeons and sparrows , that waited at a distance for their meals and then greedily swooped down upon them. The wild-pigeon is a foolish and fearful bird, flying off in panic whenever I would appear at the window and landing once I had poured out the seeds and retreated. All of the grandchildren, the ones that still needed to be carried, or those who could already stand on stools or chairs and see for themselves, got used to the sight as part of their grandmother's routine. Sometimes a pair of bulbuls joined in.

Some of the ravens that were a permanent fixture on the palm tree tried to swipe the food, but didn't find the birdseed satisfying, and once in a while they managed to steal a slice of the wet bread that I would place in a separate container for the sparrows.

I didn't bond with the wild-pigeons but I considered myself responsible for them. For years they nested on the porch or near it, laying their eggs and giving the apartment an air of permanence and harmony with its surroundings. I still missed the falcons that had adopted me.

The large ficus tree across the street blocked the light and the sea breeze, but sometimes flocks of birds perched on it. They would land, busily and noisily in a whirlwind dance, loudly descending upon the tree with nightfall. When my eyes adjusted to the darkness, I could make out the fruit-bats unlatching themselves from the ficus branches, flying like well-aimed arrows, dropping spittle and excrement on the white walls. In the morning there were flocks of swallows on it, a few blackbirds and a stubborn woodpecker. The pigeons and the sparrows would position themselves on its branches or along the electricity line, waiting with dull expectation for their daily bird seed, and I would scatter the seeds, stand back and leave them to nourish their bodies.

Leaving the apartment that I sold meant parting with the birds and plants too. The woman who purchased the apartment received a lengthy description of my daily routine with the birds, although I knew they would survive without the luxury of being fed. The jasmine, however, would never make it through the summer without meticulous care.

The flight paths of the neighborhood birds were a major consideration in my search for a new apartment. I also checked the amount of light and shade for the plants that would envelop me, the direction of the wind and the hours of daylight, I searched patiently for the last parking spot in my life, shedding all that is superfluous and reinforcing my will to be protected from the obstacles of my heavy gait, a refuge that would ease the longing that congests the end of the road.

A longing for what has passed and can never return, and for the desires that will remain unfulfilled.

Moving meant parting from whatever remained. A few necessary provisions were taken for the journey to the end. The contents of the locked room and its secrets, as well as the fascination with a different sort of winged creature, the swift. A bird that is in flight more than any other in nature. For most of its life, the swift is airborne and doesn't land, except to nest. In a single continuous flight it eats, wakes, sleeps, mates, rests and hunts. It's faster than any other bird– catching insects and ingesting them while still in the air. It has no need or desire to stop, lean, land, cling to a branch or a twig or a piece of land. Swifts are in flight from the day that they hatch until they reach sexual maturation, when they mate –monogamously– and nest in the cracks of old buildings, ancient walls (there are 88 nests mapped in the Western Wall) or other hiding places that they can frequent without requiring the momentum of a low take-off point. They take-off in droves for their massive migration, until the cycle of mating and nesting season repeats once more. Hovering on air currents, suspended over continents in the search for warmth, insects, mates and flocks– all at great heights, in complete freedom for their entire lives. It is a frantic, playful mode of existence that both attracts and unnerves me. A carefree life without territorial definitions and set boundaries.

I am captivated by their lack of dependence, they are there and I am here. I follow their actions with awe and am a member of the Friends of the Swifts Society. I watch anxiously as the flock carries out their complicated maneuvers and hold my breath when I am sure that a collision is imminent as they take off or swerve between buildings. They are in their own world. They do not know that there are countless articles written about them; they are not part of the permanent fabric of my reciprocal relationships with nature, I observe the endless cycle constantly passing above me, it leaves no footprint on the ground, has different concepts of time, space and gravity, exhaling with relief when they leave at the beginning of summer, disappearing from the vast open sky above the balcony of my new apartment.

In my new apartment looking out on the square, like the movement of the sun, I have turned my back to the salty ocean breeze and now face eastwards, the over-sized windows and automated blinds control the light and the darkness, the heat and the drafts as well as the birds and plants.

I feel that being in the high, open space in the new apartment counters the marginality I that has been forced upon me. The responsibility remains the same. The activities and the quickness of response were undertaken according to my limited capacity, and the echo of my own voice beckoning, protesting, offering, undermining, was weaker. Perhaps my confidence was too. Not in the justice of the convictions but in my ability to carry them out. The white dove of peace pinned to my lapel, the same responses, the same rhetoric, refusing to admit the sense of frustration that had spread through my body. Disappointed, not victorious, but not obstructing any paths or hopes.

In the new apartment there are new horizons and there is a different kind of greenery, reddish floors, blue railings and high ceilings but the further I see from here, the more clearly I can comprehend the dwindling emotional resources and my inability to fortify them. It's not withdrawal and surrender, but a more sober, cautious stance, searching for pathways to avoid the pitfalls that have piled up on the road that I still regard as the only viable option. The political, national and moral responsibility to resolve the bloody conflict has not deviated but has been engraved in stone, a pure solemn oath, unspoiled by the moment, an oath that I wanted to live by and not die with.

Despite the doubts and misgivings that accompanied the new place, its purchase, renovations and the move – I feel like a dethroned queen in her own fortress of satisfaction and comfort. I upgrade the constraints, lining them with resigned tolerance.

I decide to lure the birds to my doorstep again, and among the plants that I select in colors and heights that suit my taste, I make sure to include some whose nectar is a favorite of the birds.

The city's *Department for Urban Beautification* published an *Informative List of Bird-and Butterfly-Attracting Plants*. The guide is comprised of eight tables and it had all of the information I needed: name of plant/ form of growth/season/colour/light/ bird or butterfly it attracts/ etc., and accordingly: "Veronica Spicata/ Herbaceous/ 50-60 cm/Spring-Summer/ White/ Pink/ Blue/ Direct Sunlight/ Honey-sucker/ Sensitive to Dryness."

I sow and plant to attract honey-suckers and butterflies, whether in shade or direct sunlight, agapanthus and hibiscus, sweet clover and rosalia. Fresh earth, two water dispensers for the honey-suckers– artificial flowers that contain sugar water– planting carefully, taking into consideration directions and seasons, and paying utmost attention to professional guidance: "The bower vine, Pandorea Jasminoides, not to be confused with a common trumpet creeper." There's no chance I would ever mistake a pandorea for a trumpet creeper, or that I would mislead the honey-suckers and the butterflies.

And they came. A playful pair of honey-suckers, a turquoise, bright blue male and a grayish-brown female they were attracted by the sugar-water and the red pentas flowers which bloomed in all of their glory. Every morning they leap and chirp from flower to flower until they have satisfied their hunger and quenched their thirst.

The honey-suckers do not look at me, neither in suspicion nor in fear. I watch them and we strike up a one-sided relationship; on my side there is love, care and careful attention from afar. They're not for petting or a mutual attraction or dependence. If the hibiscus and the agapanthus wilt, they will find another porch with jasmine and malvaviscus. If I am no longer here, the same thing that occurred in my other apartment will happen here as well– whoever takes my place might have to make do with restless swifts or the ring-necked parakeets that pierce the silence with their shrieks like overbearing invaders. Watching because they enter your field of vision and not because you are looking for them.

I bond with plants in a different manner. The choice is mine. The color schemes, fragrance, taste, painting each window box and striking a balance between the various heights, the different shades of the leaves and the changing seasons all necessitate precision in planting the bulbs and corms, pruning the roses and weeding the annual plants when their season is up, all of which comes with the sorrow of the end of a cycle of life.

The passion I have for different patterns of colors, scents and the sweetness of nectar, far surpasses the limited space that I have at my disposal in the deep planters facing east and west. I am frustrated that I cannot contain them all even if I plant annuals and double the variety, and disperse the seeds of the lower standing flowers within the taller ones. And how many rows should I plant? In one there are low adaptable plants that trail downwards, and in another row there are low standing ones, and in the one by the railing there are all sorts of climber plants and creepers and in between the planters– in the space between them– potted plants for the creepers that ascend the building's wall, wrapping themselves around air conditioning hoses and even, out of the kindness of my heart, flowering on the balconies of the neighboring apartments.

In the kitchen window facing west there is a herb and spice window box: bush basil, "magic mountain" with purple blossoms that the honey-sucker is particularly fond of, cherry tomatoes, hyssop, mint, white savory, sage, rosemary and thyme– all of them are used in my kitchen.

The window boxes facing east are on full display for passersby on the boulevard and the square below, they look up in appreciation, for it is the only thing blooming in the row of plain, disheveled buildings.

Chapter 3

Was writing my real call? Why the thirty-five years interval between two books?
Was the status of "A provocative politician" an excuse? Ill health an alibi ?

You draw a line between the subjects you want to write about. You hesitate, pausing between one line and another, but your hesitation has no trace of a question. Your last book was published thirty years ago, three years after the death of your father.[5] Dov's illness was diagnosed as incurable Parkinson's disease and the symptoms began appearing, fortunately slowly, but they limited his ability to function and pierced their way through to the perimeter of your life. The hand that grips the pen and fills the blank pages did not cease its activity, but you turned instead to writing articles and essays, to jousting with rivals and the accomplishments in your political and social life led to a deeper involvement, a move from writing to taking action, from the squares and left- wing protest groups to campaigning for a seat in the *Knesset*.

You have been running scenarios through your head for eleven years. Stories and essays and chapters of your life and emotions and actions have been recorded on scraps of paper, so you wouldn't forget the people, the loves or the details of poignant and moving stories. You trust the process of natural selection in your thoughts and emotions and rarely write an entire paragraph, chapter or a full thought, for your notes are not intended for publication. Even the most intimate, painful, hurtful things that will never be published are written concisely and make their way to the locked room that still accompanies you, subsuming the turmoil that you keep to yourself, the painful shortcomings that you have as a woman, a mother, a wife, a sister and a daughter.

For a decade you travel between your home and the *Knesset*, between Dov's illness, the lives of your children, and the complex legislative acts that sometimes succeed in eliminating obstacles and manage to move mountains. You juggle between the two paths.

Dov's illness gets progressively worse and your public work is successful, and as you try to accommodate both worlds, the enjoyable act of creative writing that you crave

---

5 Yael Dayan, *My Father, His Daughter.*

is trapped and wears down.

The silence, patience, equanimity and limitless time remain out of reach and you tell yourself: afterwards, during the *Knesset* recess, in the next term, and the things that you wanted to write during those years are so personal, so wracked with guilt, sailing off to forbidden or far-reaching waters that you do not even dare write and bury them, like you did when the letters you wrote were surely destroyed, just as you did not trust the locked drawers and destroyed their responses.

It's been almost a decade since Dov died, my life continued on its course of public service, the responsibility and devotion left little room for quietude, concentration and my spare time was lovingly dedicated to my grandchildren. But the more I dealt with speculations about my own death, its imminent proximity and the decline of my vitality, the stronger the urge and ability to write grew. This awareness looms over my life, sets boundaries to my sleep patterns, calculates the time remaining, defines all that I will never have a chance to do and alters my standards. At the same time, I also experience memory lapses.

Forgetfulness violently erases the possibility to glean and save information. It chills my blood. Terrifying. I try to sort it into different categories. The freezing standstill when I try to extract a name that is on the tip of my tongue or at the front of my brain, but still cannot utter it. The minor stroke that I had on the *Knesset* podium was a pre-liminary, elusive sign. It occurred during my second term, the *Knesset* hall was silent, and I was proposing a bill that was likely to pass, entitled "The Prevention of Stalking" which was at the final stages of its proposition. I read one line and felt myself choking on the words. I tried again and couldn't string two words together. My friend Noef Masalcha was the Chairperson at the time and he noticed my distress. He read the bill in my place and called for a doctor and held the vote on the bill that was eventually passed— as expected. The doctor gave me sweet tea and aspirin, I felt a slight paralysis in my arm, I could speak again but the numb sensation in my mouth lingered for a few minutes longer. By the time I reached Hadassah Medical Center and underwent an MRI, the stroke was already over, having evaded the scan and leaving no traces in the magnetic field, or virtually none, apart from the unforgettable experience and the chilling reminder of the twilight awaiting me. They kept me at the hospital that night for observation and I left feeling apprehensive at the prospect of another stroke that could happen unexpectedly when I was alone. Blood thinners were added to my list of medications and I was sent on my way. Lately the fear has risen up again. I find it hard to "extract" a piece of information that has not been forgotten but remains lodged somewhere and refuses to budge. It is mainly names, I can remember last names but not first, the first syllable but not the last, sometimes failing to remember numbers or names of places.

The forgotten piece of information always returns to me, breaking through the fog a few minutes later, but it only occurs when I stop exerting myself with attempts to remember. As characteristic of the elderly, I am apologetic, embarrassed by my forgetfulness, "At my age, you start to go senile…" and very afraid. I exercise my mind. Memory games, cryptic crossword puzzles, names of classmates and members of my military squad in basic training, IDF major-generals, Bible verses that we learned by heart as children, the poetry of Nathan Alterman, Dahlia, entire books. And still, it happens, and I resort to memory-saving to-do lists, whom to call, what to prepare, and then— where have I put the list? This kind of forgetfulness doesn't bother me. I know that it is temporary, the names will return, the faces will rejoin their rightful names and the numbers will return from their evil ways.

The real source of terror is the loss of entire chapters of life. The tip of the iceberg floats innocently in the depths of my mind, yet I am unable to dive down and reach it. I am Ariadne, caught in a maze, and the thread that I have in my hand has come loose and is crumbling, and amnesia becomes a sealed wall that I cannot break out of to step into freedom.

I try to minimize the fear of the blanks and empty spaces that appear on my patchy brainscan. This isn't happening to me. There is no solace in the obliteration of the hardships and failures, nor in the memory which is a blow to humanity, to mankind, to me.

The memory that brings the ignorance to light, everything that we haven't learned, the memory that asks no questions, that encompasses the obvious. The memory of birth and the memory of death and the knowledge that the end is as evident as the be-ginning, like the primary division of cells, or the number of cells that break down and the neurons that are wiped out, like organ failure or disintegration. The never ending attempt to circumvent this awareness, through science-fiction, space travel, artificial insemination and cloning, through embryonic stem cells and cryonics, all in order to forget the systematic, remembered, experienced, the terrifying banality of the end.

All religions aim to compensate for the awareness of the end in order to give pur-pose to the life that will surely be taken away. Through superstition, the afterlife, immortality, heaven and hell, reincarnation and resurrection. The certainty of death debilitates free-flowing vitality, the struggle for survival against nature and its decrees. In this manner I try to remember at will or consider the memory lapses and ignorance that are mined from bottomless pits or lack clear and defined borders and attempt to mark them.

About a week ago, on a hot July day, Victoria-Catherina Pötzel, a PhD student from the University of Vienna came to see me. We had corresponded over email and I accepted her request to interview me as part of her thesis *The Literature/Books of Yael Dayan*. Ms. Pötzel looked exactly as I had pictured her. Rail thin, blonde and blue-eyed, in a long sleeveless black dress that revealed skin so pale it rarely, if ever, saw the sun. As I prepared chicken for our lunch, it occurred to me that perhaps I should've inquired about her food preferences, and almost as expected-— too late— I found out that she is a vegetarian.

Between helpings of salad, fruit, bread and olives, we reached what was for me, the embarrassing part. Victoria was well-prepared, a diligent, meticulous and thorough student, she had drawn up a series of questions and introductions from all of my books. It would not be an exaggeration to say that she could very well have been speaking about another author whom I haven't read, and my embarrassment was due to my utter lack of identification with the material. How young I was, I thought, searching for words and neatly arranging them. We spoke in English and she quoted from my books in English, and the thesis will be written in Austrian German.

I tried to be somewhat provocative and find amusement in the rippling of the waves without taking a chance and delving deep, for fear of capsizing and drowning. I made a few remarks when required, I tried to reconstruct– and that turned out well –why I wrote and what I wanted to say, and the reason behind my attempt to debunk myths and perhaps to create others, less rigid, with broader horizons and even some that have failed and only the story remains, a dangling skeleton, like an empty sound box where the nothingness crashed within them and justified the erasure of the myths from the slabs of memory.

When she left, satisfied, I wondered whether all writers remember their works forty or fifty years later and what the relationship is between memory and quality. Do I forget the fictional and tend to remember the factual incidents of my life that were woven into the works? A work that was purely fictional, and the best of my books – *Death Had Two Sons* – lacks all biographical traces, it was all researched, examined and sensed down to my very core and has not faded or been forgotten, but nonetheless, I still would have written it differently, as if to say I would have lived my life differently, not the course of it or its geographical location, but a different distribution of time, the time of the living and the time of the dead, arranging them at alternative distances on the pathways.

In the year that I am describing, I am 73-4 years old. I have changed my address and opened up over-sized windows to the east, turned my back to the sea breeze and the setting sun, and moved from a large, closed-in space to a smaller, colorful and wide expanse, where I inescapably face myself, where I have grown aware of the evident deficiencies that were once part of my daily existence.

Broadening and updating my knowledge – reaching for the shrouded secrets of science and the future, writing again, daring to replace Dahlia's eyes and intellect with another gaze, keeping my soul from despair, from the banal, the insipid, the glaring open pit.

Hanging on to the slope of time by my fingernails, soon I will have had more of the decline of the lungs and the dead neurons in my brain, and I will cease to be.

Instantaneously.

I began a new decade when I moved. The previous one consisted of the change from the *Knesset* and my Jerusalem days to the new home base in Tel-Aviv. My failure in the last *Knesset* elections, my success in the campaign for city council, the depressing standstill– which did not deter my optimism and the desperate, but futile attempts up until this point– in advancing the peace process, the old-new public life. I plunged into the waters of "civilian life" with the birth of my grandchildren, when my life took on a meaning that stemmed from its quality, rather than a promise of longevity.

The deaths of Dov and Dahlia had flattened out my horizon and my will to live, the heaviness of the time remaining, all these were pushed aside to make room for these four children who came into my crippled world and ignited it with meaning and light.

And why do you live as if on borrowed time? The self-pity, the frequent silent sympathy, as if you are accompanying yourself to the final bad place. You list your losses and revive the memories that fail to overcome you with emotion; they appear, floating by, they are abrasive, misshapen, and do not provide shelter. You regret the missed opportunities more than you revel in the successes. A void surrounds you and sometimes a crack opens up, sucking you in– the grandchildren, a delightful play, an enthralling book, and the cracks are always beckoning but they do not bring with them the hope of reconciliation, of peace, of a dream coming true be it even when you are gone. You are inflicted with the pain of deficient knowledge, education, of belated beginnings, of a relationship that ended relatively early, and all the remembered and forgotten things that were not exhausted. Some of them remain in the locked room, not because of secrecy or shame but due to fear. You are afraid of discovering the depths of the loves that you dismissed, afraid to admit the unnecessary provocation of your friends and parents, hiding the actions that you regretted, the mistakes that you didn't mend even when you had the chance. The prices you paid.

You lived by leaps and bounds– from mountaintop to mountaintop, off the diving board into stormy waters, sailing the restless waves.

And making emergency landings. Grasping at buoys or knots and floating onwards, reaching the safety of the shore when it was already too late and you were not strong enough to start afresh on to a new runway and take off.

During the course of this year, in the new apartment flooded with light, I have awakened from the habitual proximity of death and even the desire to hasten it, to an acceptance of a limited life, as the body does not heed to me and I struggle and let go over and over again, in pain, tiring of it, then returning, trying once again, pushing the grievances into the locked room, with the failed relationships with my daughter and son and my reflection in the mirror that magnifies the wrinkles and the brown age-stains.

I gather sufficient strength to engage in the struggle against the occupation and the seemingly hopeless efforts to replace the certainty of war by the hopes for peace.

I manage the loneliness by performing small, personal rituals. A meal served on a tray with a folded linen napkin, beautiful dishes, a glass of wine. A lavender-scented bubble bath, a long soak and an over-sized white towel, delicate nightgowns and all sorts of indulgences that end, every night, with a volume of poetry– Dahlia's poems, Szymborska and Milosz, the poems of Sylvia Plath and William Blake– poems of darkness that do not calm the nerves, but enchant, sprouting wings even when the pain is greater than the joy. They differ from the exciting and inspiring poetry that I read by day. Nathan Zach and Yitzhak Laor, the love poems of Ori Bernstein, Cavafy, Dylan Thomas, T.S.Eliot, and Nathan Alterman, always Alterman, stirring memories and my longing for the person I used to be and the one I wanted to be, manifesting disheartening sorrows and shadows in the recesses that are only visible, after all, when the sun shines, and the colors of the blossoms are bright.

Tending to the window box garden has its highs and lows.

The jasmine leaves yellowed, the roses are infested with whiteflies, the pentas need pruning and the purple lobelia are done blooming for the season. A dense forest of basil fills the kitchen window box, facing west, the white-leaved savory sends its thin, spotted arms to meet the bare fingers of the pink gaura. I shed all pretense to fight botanical odds.

I take pleasure in each meticulously cared for corner of the house and every embroidered pillow or sculpture made by my brother Udi, in the paintings that look back at me every day of the year and have not lost their radiance. This small space also provides me with unintentional distractions and excuses, as I am well-aware, filling my days and nights with minor activities, preventing me from turning to writing with the same urgency and passion I once had.

Fifty years ago and more, when I had all the time I now lack, and the vitality that the years have dulled, when everything indicated that I would have the chance to study and write as well, become a scientist and an intellectual, a public figure and a serious thinker adopting as my mentors Buber, Agnon, Nitzsche, as well as Tolstoy and Kafka, Freud and Sartre–whom I read voraciously and almost indiscriminately.

Followed the decades spent scaling barricades with all of my might. Absorbing the blows and the abuse, shouting the slogans and carrying the picket signs, making speeches and distributing stickers in the squares and in the intersections .Active in the marches and vigils, tramping through the off-limit zones, in all languages, carried away with my fervor and persuading others in my firm belief in justice and peace. All under the thick cloud of occupation, sealed to prayers and logic.

Personal encounters reinforced me with effortless charm, and I fostered agreeable, inquisitive relationships, never sensing that I was setting a fixed course, and not realizing that the path I left behind would be blocked if I didn't take it. I felt omnipotent at the time.

I focused comfortably on the two complementary spheres of creativity and the imagination, the same limitless space that can expand and contract according to your will. Literature, poetry, art, philosophy and the more tangible, rational world is closer to home, illuminated and easy for me to grasp. History and political science, conflict resolution and human rights, the legal and justice system, a light that is simple to try and grasp. Addicted to studying, working, creating and contributing my part in the giant mosaic as if there is no end and no tomorrow, and death is merely another thought or concept rather than a documented and terrifying physical certainty.

I haven't reached the lighthouse that lies at the top of that mountain yet, but I had the tools to climb it. Knowledge that was both innate and actively acquired, with soul-expanding joy, diligence, intuition, I was blessed with a sharp memory and a fullness of conviction in the path of progress, or at least, the educated strive towards it.

The other sphere, that which is quantifiable and in part, tangible and proven, hidden and enticing, revealed itself to me belatedly, when I was unequipped to comprehend and grasp it.

The realm of science is to me the field of my desperate ignorance and irreparable illiteracy. The road I will never travel.

In my immediate family there were no scientists, doctors, mathematicians, nor was anyone inclined towards science or any of its appendages. For me, deep scientific inquiry and its implications were part of the unknown and remained unattainable, and I applied myself rigorously to the humanities and social studies. I felt that my "aptitude" was poor and that I lacked the "talent" to deal with the quantifiable and its diagrams, and to the systems and numbers that pertained to physics and chemistry. My personal and formal education was limited to vague notions and my comprehension was that of a reasonable person, comprised of basic scholastic requirements. I asked the right questions, I contemplated, I made mistakes and searched the parameters of perceptible entities, both conscious and subconscious, in psychology, sociology and ethics, in systems of government and legal matters, in wars and peace accords, in literary manifestations, documents and in the poetry that infused them all with emotion and stirred me deeply.

I skipped over a form of knowledge and its absence now plagues me like a deep thirst for water and a hunger for bread; I realize that I will never be able to satisfy it in the time remaining. Questions about the origin of mankind, the essence of existence, the particles that comprise the cells that make up the organisms that form the entirety that is part of a system that communicates with its various parts and with other systems, and nowadays everything can be mapped out and simulated, and nature can be substituted, and we are almost (just almost) on the verge of the secret of life itself, its creation– and inevitable annihilation. I woke up to all of this after writing five books in the course of a decade. I moved in international, multi-cultural, creative, rebellious and innovative circles post–WWII, a time when the national and personal reckonings were coming to an end, with the morose, bleak, and brilliant-to-the-very-depths-of-despair works of Camus, Paul Celan, Elie Wiesel, Primo Levi. We sat in the gray remnants of smoke and we brushed against the talkative or silent survivors. We dared to smile again, to love and to be exuberant, excited at the vitality of existence and sex, lead by Hemingway, de Beauvoir, Tennessee Williams and the literature of the American South, buoyed by the art of French cinema and English theatre and the Beatles, everyone promised something new. I felt that I was part of a world that was rapidly moving in a positive direction. A dynamic, familiar world that rested in the palm of my hand. Israel, my birthplace, was young and struggling, seemingly provincial and undefined as yet. It had the luster of novelty, the freshness of innocence and the self-centered air of the righteous.

In 1962, Watson, Crick and Wilkins received the Nobel Prize in Physiology or

Yael Dayan

Medicine. I read *The Double Helix* twice and must've sensed that it would turn my life upside down. Gone was the sense that the entire world rested in the palm of my hand. The hand was empty, and the sphere rolled off into closed other territories, off-limits. And ever since, I have been searching for a small crack to look through or a partial understanding or a byroad to take so I can touch the mystery, or at least the promise of incredible, expansive solutions put forth for mankind and its researchers. My sense of security has been undermined and I try to patch gigantic holes and seal huge bottomless pits by throwing crumbs at them. I gather them in handfuls, they slip through my fingers and I regain my peace of mind by collecting the crystal flakes that rapidly evaporate. I cannot do it. It's too late. I do not have enough to even define myself as anything more complex than a mass of decomposable energy. My pathetic attempts to bridge gaps and restore inadequacies and improve on that which has been tarnished in the margins and feed the curiosity that has not waned, have met with little success. The more I learn, the more the colossal disparity between what I acquire and what I lack becomes apparent. I am shamed by my ignorance. My inquisitiveness is depressing because the slope is steep and, at the top of the mountain I can see more summits in the distance and in order to reach them, I will have to go down to the depths and gather my strength, quench my thirst, strengthen my muscles and climb. Again and again.

Before my military service and prior to the publication of my first book, my father thought I should study agronomy, zoology or botany. He accepted my decision to take up a different field and we even shared a university course, he would unabashedly talk to me during the exams– in a low whisper–and our professors were forgiving and ignored our mutual chirps of assistance. Whoever noticed could see that I always sat to his right, beside the seeing eye. Only a decade later– after two wars, two great loves and a host of romantic deliberations–did I stop to consider the missed opportunities, the understanding that it was too late. I would not study medicine or biochemistry, and I found tremendous satisfaction in my life and my marriage and joy in motherhood. I managed to face challenges head-on and accomplish personal and public goals that were far from the main issue that I had repressed–the ephemeral nature of our existence. Our existence as tiny particles that are part of a huge unknown whose purpose is not comprehensible to me, if it indeed has a purpose beyond preserving itself and that too does not lie in the realm of consciousness. The relativity dwarfed the joys and the sorrows, the triumphs and the tribulations. But then Dov's illness struck, bringing with it the complete finality, and that decade brought me back to the subjects I had been preoccupied with– the complexity of the brain, dopamine and the MRI.

Dov's inevitable deterioration was further motivation to advance and deepen my search. His illness and our means of coping with it also led me to contemplate the fields that I had missed out on, the ones I did not sow and reap and which still remain out of reach.

Years before, I had studied life sciences at the Open University for a lengthy period of time. I applied myself with the rigor of a high-school student. The material was new and challenging, but I was able to tap into a wellspring of focus and interest and I mailed in my exams, participated in the lab experiments and lectures; I loved *The Philosophy of Science* and I raised drosophila flies in test tubes, comparing the males to the females and their wingspans, pouring over the mysteries of basic genetics, which was the subject I was most interested in. Evolution and genetics– long after Darwin and Mendel and before the double helix and the mapping of the genome– professions that inspire, are free-thinking, provide room for original thought have always fascinated me. When I reached chemistry and biochemistry I dropped out due to lack of interest– not in the cell or cytology but lack of interest in the molecules and the connection between them. Mathematical thinking and computer programming were beyond me, although I undoubtedly had a natural gift for foreign languages, which I would pick up "by the wayside" without any formal study.

Evolution and genetics. The connection between them continues to occupy my thoughts and enrich my body of knowledge. My curiosity and the urge to know is awakened whenever something real torments me, and then the urge transforms into a need that does not heed to barriers and will not tolerate any murky misunderstandings. That was how I researched Dov's illness– the medication, the numerous studies conducted on various forms of Parkinson's disease, identifying the stages of deterioration– in the attempt to fight the disease and create optimal conditions for delaying it, and also to hide the truth from him.

When I was diagnosed with breast cancer, I had another opportunity to research the wondrous field of medicine that I missed out on. I chose to know everything and embark on the path of treatment, surgery and recovery by myself, and in time another malignancy was discovered in my breast and I underwent surgery and radiation for the second time and ever since I have been closely monitored and examined every six months. At present, and for the next five-years, I am considered cancer-free, yet all of the benchmarks in my life changed and I began to cool-headedly calculate the end, mocking my sense of long-term security in the very state of existence.

Nowadays, any way I count it, most of my life has already passed, and the number of years I have left interests me in terms of the general ramifications– impending war, hunger, three-dimensional printing, lifespan control, the existence of life on other planets–huge waves of immigration from Africa to Europe and from the Far East to Australia ,reshaping cultures and the global economy rather than the chain of my own personal events.

Counting the years remaining for my mother is another matter, and it is separate from my own, for she is graced with positive, rewarding determination that is consistently present in every day of her life, and it's hard to speculate which one of us will die first, me with my failing health and slackening desire to get up in the morning, or my mother, approaching her centennial birthday–who has a certain degree of fatigue, but whose days are filled with work and a never-ending hope for a better day tomorrow– or will it be my younger brother, whose life should have ended years ago according to every law of nature, as his brain, veins and lungs have been fed every kind of toxin available, and the blanks and spots in the grey matter on his CT scan indicated that he would likely be subject to life-shortening behavioral disruptions.

My chronic obstructive lung disease (COPD), an incurable ailment, didn't spark any scientific interest, but merely the attempt to cope and handle the incapacity that it causes. A misfortune that I want to withstand. I tried to ignore and push it aside more than understand or research it. The doctors sum it up as a chronic decrease of lung capacity.

The damages caused by smoking have turned into a serious obstructive lung disease, which has gotten progressively worse, and the percentage of active lung tissue has dropped irreversibly. Inhalers of all sorts, a shortness of breath after taking merely a few steps, and for balance– a wheelchair, an oxygen concentrator, a portable oxygen machine, these devices have become permanent fixtures in my life whenever I want to travel, eat out, work, and sometimes while driving or spending time with my grandchildren. Oxygen tubes stuck in my nostrils when I'm on the street, children look on curiously and passersby don sympathetic expressions. The failure of medicine to offer a true remedy for the third deadliest disease worldwide.

There is also the dissatisfaction from the very change of pace and resolving myself to the thought of what I will never be able to do, the loves that will remain unrealized and the dreams that will never be pursued. The pitiful attempt to give off an air of "business as usual". Smiles, photographs ,back to the relativity of things.

When I was in pain I didn't dare complain or cry in the presence of others. And Dov is not here to lean on.

"So what restrains me?
Shame That my misfortunes are not colorful enough?" [6]

And always, besides the lack of oxygen and chronic lung failure, I suffer from what is not plain to the eye and has no medical definition. The loss of neurons, the shortening of telomeres with age, writing reminders to myself.

Strangers would not notice the frail bones and the slackness of the skin in the private parts, nor could they surmise that the parting from the desires of the flesh cannot be replaced with emotional fortitude–even if I had it. Preserving that which remains instead of expanding it, temporarily patching up faded spots for the sake of appearances. Without faking . Nevertheless, I do not cease to gather information and knowledge and fill in the blanks and the emptiness, treading on the bridges and taking shortcuts that bow under the weight of my hesitant ignorance, knowing a little about everything or a lot about a little, the two tasks being impossible, of course.

---

6 Czeslaw Milosz "Prescription".

Chapter 4

Username. Password. Delete. Years 2000...

I resume writing and the distractions from other fields seem to multiply. As if I have to earn the right or pay a fine in order to write, to express, put into words, restrict or reveal myself.

In my public duties–in the office I handle various matters successfully. I can renovate plans, improve tactics ,aid and be of help. And I act vigorously, persistent and practical. I can sense the brain cells gaping open in their desire to soak up, to store with urgency, to connect the different parts into a single continuum of knowledge and communicate amongst themselves, clusters of neurons, waterfalls of assemblages, receptors and neurotransmitters, seeing the entire puzzle come together if only in a single small piece–I build up confidence in my ability to concentrate, to retain and comprehend knowledge. I test myself all the time.

The choice was yours and you made it. You didn't complete your higher education, you didn't pursue sciences that necessitated precision and thoroughness, you were lazy and recited poetry– effortlessly and with great pleasure– rather than equations, you made due with formulating the right questions rather than attempting to answer them, and later, the ease and delight that you found in the act of writing, the independence and freedom to take on different roles and cast yourself in a variety of characters and float off, gathering the nectar and experiences without any use for anchors or footholds. You made your choice and now you know that you cannot undo it. It was within your power, had you made the effort, you could have taken both paths. You could have sought further and not made due with the ripe fruit that fell into your lap.

Chekhov, Bulgakov and Williams Carol Williams were doctors.There were renowned scientists who were also philosophers and founded trends of philosophy and ethics. Many doctors that you knew played classical music in some quartet or another and wrote poetry, but your years overflowed with no real peaks, without ascending to great heights or tumbling down to the depths. You hurt people, you toyed with their emotions in your youth, testing the boundaries and trifling with the edge without falling in, and through it all, whether due to an innate or acquired understanding, you retained a sense of integrity that constituted a solid backbone, which you then could offer to those in need.

And now the restlessness of a perfectionist is all that remains. It is a slow journey to the end of the road, to an attempt to reach some kind of home stretch that constitutes a small, true statement, ending "..not with a bang but a whimper." [7]

And what prevents you from smiling and emitting a slow, calm, final sigh?

Slow? Calm? The sound is of hammers pounding in the electronic, digital maze, post- everything, expose-everything, with insanity inducing noise, the telephone twists the senses and infiltrates every aspect of identity with its bleeps and notifications and alerts, with its flashing, vibrating and texting and the new language that lacks musicality and soaks everything in violent vulgarity, with all-purpose cellular devices, unsophisticated answers to questions and an automated response system that neutralizes any question we wanted to ask with a web of options plus the ability to return to the "main menu" where we are led through the labyrinth to insanity, ad nauseam, ad infinitum.

Grosso Modo is it a blessing or a curse? The question is asked by those nostalgic for simplicity, rejecting the loud cacophony. Scientists that may know what the future holds, but do not know where to stop in the present, experts on ethics who wish to examine progress rationally and set new moral boundaries, politicians who trust their ability to delineate boundaries within the framework of the systems of government known to us– they usually originate progress, development and innovation in addition to being the sources of their funding and implementation.

There doesn't seem to be a self-destruct mechanism beyond a certain limit and no future index that can predict where progress will lead, even when placed in well-meaning democratic hands. There are benefits to the life sciences, computing, creating models that can diagnose and track the flaws, developing alternative energy solutions and assessing predictions of preventable accidents. But how much choice do we actually have?

I revisit my thoughts in adolescence. How much of our experience, our mature personality, is preordained, determined by genetic structure, or even by education and the environment? And how much of us constitutes the mind unleashed, free will, choice, is located above water and in our hands. And do we have an "added value" in our genetic make-up, a sliver of freedom that separates us, an atom that we have caught and which generates free will, and does free will exist in clones that are designed by a computer/human robot or by perfect material cloning, in which case what would then be its source?

Will the creature be able to choose freely, or perhaps it is the other way around, maybe science will enslave us, flawlessly programming us to think that the choice and freedom are in our hands while both are located in our programming. And will the

---

7 T.S. Eliot "The Hollow Men."

relationship between the blessing and the curse then be undermined?

Will what is flawlessly programmed contain the possibility of deception as well? And perhaps we are already the product of cloning, or exist amongst the products of cloning in a parallel universe and we have been implanted with the ability to err?

The pounding and hammering from ear to ear and head to toe is relentless. I want to wait for the mailman, to hopefully and enthusiastically anticipate the "bearer of letters." To use a fountain pen and write a response six to eight pages long on thin sheets of paper, perhaps perfume it, fold it, place it in an envelope, seal it, put a stamp and print "airmail" on it and walk to the post office and drop the letter in the box.

Ready-made airmail envelopes used to be too small and thus "airmail" needed to be printed on the envelope in order for your letter to avoid being shipped by sea, a journey that took several weeks. We collected stamps and postcards from foreign and exotic places and saved them in albums that have since yellowed and faded. Grandpa Shmuel dated every photograph and described it at length. Photographs in the "Workers Union" or "Degania" or in *Nahalal* or in "The First *Knesset*"— standing from right...seated....kneeling...S. Dayan, D. Dayan, Z. Shazar, P. Sapir, D. Ben-Gurion.

From high school on, a trickle of love notes started to appear, as well as the occasional love letter. I sent letters in cuneiform characters to a teacher whose attention I sought and got a response in ancient Accadian. The teacher died since and the letters reached me. They are in the locked room though there is no way I could decipher them now.

The diary that I kept in high school ended badly. I wrote a combination of fact and fiction and my father found it in my room and paid no attention to my explanations about the difference between the two. What ensued was a slap in the face, an apology from him and the destruction of my pages.

Our telephone number at home in Jerusalem was comprised of four digits–3609. Grandma and grandpa's was 4741. They were all easy to remember and didn't have codes or complications, not even the hot line connecting father and the head of the Jordanian Legion. There was a rotary dialer, no choice of ring-tones and the phone, alarm clock and sometimes even the school bell had the same ring.

My grandmother and grandfather, Shmuel and Dvora, exchanged letters and saved their correspondences. My father passed them on to me– without having read their handwritten letters, binders full of them, and I kept the intimate ones and donated the rest to various historical archives. Some of the ones that I kept– Grandma Dvora's– are eloquently written in Russian, which was her mother tongue, and Shmuel's are in Yiddish, he had no command of literary Russian. Eventually all of their correspondence shifted to Hebrew, his is written in dense calligraphy and hers in the round handwriting of a student.

During the final month of her life, grandfather sat at her bedside and jotted down her words– opinions, bits and pieces of Zionism, expressions of suffering that were devoid of self-pity, judgmental statements about us all. I wonder how many of the words were actually uttered by her and how many were added by my grandfather, who considered himself a documenter of Zionist life, recording his life's work and that of those around him.

When they weren't together, my parents wrote letters. I have the letters mother wrote from *Nahalal* when I was two years old, and from various other places, in addition to a collection of letters from father to me, mother to me, and the ones I wrote to them while I was travelling. There are the chapters of our lives that have been written and presented to the public, father in his autobiographical books and mother in hers, And Perhaps...and My Ruthie, a collection of letters that father wrote to her during the two years he was imprisoned at Akko (Acre) Prison.[8]

I do not know if my brothers keep bundles of letters from our parents, but the main point is the act of writing them, not saving them or the influence that they may have had on the person who received them.

I wrote and was written to throughout the years. I received love letters, letters of desperation, courtship and breakup. I saved some of them– all of Dov's, his diaries, for he too sought solace in writing, in the formulation of precise definitions. He had an eloquent tongue, was fluent in several languages and had good penmanship, a deep respect for words and a sense of humor.

I saved the letters written to me over the years and the ones I had good reason to hide were placed in the locked room, and sometimes, in silent sorrow, without passion or tears, they were destroyed too. Due to the nature of the relationships, the letters that I wrote to others were not kept.

My children and the members of their generation read less, wrote less and were too cautious to place their secrets and aching hearts in the hands of an addressed sheet of paper. They easily and expertly surfed the saccharine and deceitful computerized world, which can blot everything out with a single keystroke and remembers the twists and turns in their lives in mega and gigabytes, with passwords safeguarding the gates and codes unlocking their files, failing to differentiate between bank accounts, photographs of lovers or intimate confessions.

The children of my children were born to the rings of the bytes and applications. They started out well enough, with the Hebrew classics, learning to read and write at an early age. From then on they followed the acceptable norms. There wasn't a brand, a sneaker, or a series on the children's channel that didn't catch their eye, and later they took on the nervous motions of the sliding cellular screens, iPads and tablets. Not surfing, not the pursuit of knowledge, not a blessing, but an addiction that concerned me and added dismay to my love.

The older they got, the more I could discern the seeds of parental guidance that had been planted, grew and flourished, and the gifts that they received at my home, with family, or from an occasional good teacher who managed to overpower the devices and magical screens.

The more their horizons broadened and their knowledge deepened, the less room

8 Moshe Dayan was imprisoned by the British Police on October 3rd, 1939 in Acre Prison along with 43 members of the Jewish defence force Haganah. He was later released on February 16th 1941.

the blinks and flashes took up, making way for the glories of life, the rewarding cycle of the caterpillar, the blooming of bulbs in my garden, the extinction of dinosaurs, the scientific discoveries, the worlds that once existed and were established for us and the ability to tell the difference between the important and the trivial .

My mother took computer lessons at the age of ninety-six, she emails and sometimes surfs the web and she refuses to text message, or as she puts it–she will not text on the solar device. I think she purposefully gets it wrong.

My children use communication technology wisely– my son in finance and the stock exchange and my daughter, providing medical care as a pediatrician in the Pediatric Intensive Care Unit. Their children—my grandchildren– send photos to grandma and great grandma, decorating them with embellishments that they hunt for on PowerPoint and the littlest one wants to know whether I'd like to play "Angry Birds" with him and he does as he pleases with my cellular device, relishing in his victories. "You're really not good at this grandma," but nonetheless, he is willing to devote the time and has an interest in the origin of man and the flight paths of migrating birds.

I'm not addicted. I'm worn-out and exhausted.

My mother's grandfather was a chemist; he graduated the Sorbonne and immigrated to Israel, which was then Palestine, where he manufactured olive-oil based soap in the Arazim Valley.

My maternal grandmother studied chemistry as well, but did not work in the field. Grandma Dvora read me Pushkin's *Yevgeny Onegin* in Russian, which she would translate into lilting Hebrew, and father would sing "Mack the Knife" from *The Threepenny Opera*.

Many years later, father would wait with Nathan Alterman, Israel's great poet, outside of the printing press whenever Alterman had a new book printed. Father brought me Alterman's *City of the Dove* and *Summer Celebration* "hot out of the oven."

Dov would put the children to bed with Czech lullabies and his pleasant voice sang "Autumn is at the Window" in Hebrew with a musicality that our family undeniably lacked.

Perhaps what I am trying to write is not coming through clearly. It isn't the generation gap, nor is it about passing judgment or disappointments. The choices are greater now, and if you enjoy their benefits, the freedom and abundance, you must also have the tools to tell the difference between desires and needs. Between the transient and the permanent. I am already outside of the circle of free choice. I list the things that I will never be able to do. I apprehensively evaluate my capacity for storing new material and the habitat I have at my disposal is barely suitable for growing twigs, not to mention succulent fruit. No longer my ability to realize a goal and proceed to add layers to it. An undershirt, a t-shirt, long-sleeved shirt, a waistcoat, a jacket and finally a coat. I am attempting a different path now. Delving inwards, uncovering in order to discover, trying to gain access to some inner core and touch the root of the mystery, or at least experience the thrill of being near it.

The link between genetics and evolution. How far can the human brain reach, and is this life an evolutionary stage too, or is survival actually adaptation, and the role that the environment and culture play weaken the power of genes? Are we able to outsmart them, to clone and implant them? Is this due to boundless creative genius or are these abilities rooted in genes or in the combination of them?

The thought that my identity, my genes, the sum of my being, can be mapped out with precision and then simply saved on a disc and sent to me for a certain sum of money– is deadly. It could be the source of my need to cheat the inevitable, to burn the perfect disc, to disarray all the possible combinations that four notes are able to make, and leave me with the belief in the preeminence of man over the vast reserves of his own knowledge.

It is hard to find the focus, concentration and peace of mind necessary for writing. My day begins with the sound of the alarm I set on the cell phone. I am too sleepy to neatly slide the cursor to the right, so it keeps ringing until it wears itself out. The cell phone, like the computer are no friends of mine. Both are irritating with their insignificant, endless annoyances. There is a price to pay for utility.

There are circumstances that should be taken into account: the municipality of Tel Aviv-Yafo, where I am Chair of the City Council, is currently on break for the summer. Three of my grandchildren are in northern Greece on a trip to mark the eldest's Bat Mitzvah, touring a country familiar and very dear to me. My mother fell two days ago and broke her nose, bleeding; she is at home with a headache, but still going about her usual activities. All of the devices connecting me with the outside world are either faulty or damaged, including my landline phone, computer and cellular phone and the intercom that is working one-sidedly; I can hear people and buzz them in but they can't hear me. It's a kind of hostile takeover, confining me to my house in the debilitating August heat, waiting for hours for the repairman to come.

Some of the plants are wilting in shifts; they dry up and revive again, repeating the same cycle. The heat causes damage. And there are no signs or any indications of improvement in my lung capacity or my cerebellum, brainstem or other verified centers of the brain.

The telephone repairman arrives, shuts everything down and then turns everything on again, accidentally switching between phone lines and disabling the fax, before claiming that the machine itself is causing the electrical problem. A replacement is promptly found, but the new fax machine turns out to be guilty of the same offence. He announces that a "senior electrician" will call me and try to fix the phone line. In the meantime I try and get technical support for the problem with my cellular phone – the messages that I delete keep popping up again. Hundreds of old emails. I drink some water, take my medication, turn up the air conditioning despite the electrical company's suggestion to conserve energy, and listen to the radio with interest, as the program is about the nationwide polio vaccination campaign.

Emily, the wonderful caregiver that lives with me, cannot recall if she received a polio vaccination as a child. She phones her mother in the Philippines – there is a typhoon, schools are closed– her mother can't remember either and did not keep immunization records. I contact a physician friend who says I need not take the inactivated vaccine, nor the attenuated one but Emily does.

I drop the matter for now and try to call the telephone company again to get technical support. "You are seventeenth in line...unfortunately our system is busier than usual...please leave your number and we will get back to you as soon as possible." The message is repeatedly played over unbearable music. The estimated wait time is forty-three minutes.

I receive spectacular photos of my grandchildren in Greece on my phone. I am struck by nostalgia-tinged envy. I forward the photos to my daughter's in-laws and we exchange proud, satisfied messages.

The cell phone continues to beep, notifying me of outdated messages and I delete them all– from the computer, memory, hard drive, storage, internet, and by renouncing them I feel victorious. I silence all of the devices, the damaged ones and the ones still running, the digital and the programmed ones. Silence, detachment, the soothing hum of the oxygen generator as it fuses the goodness outside with the bubble in which I float restfully .

The intercom buzzes. I press the button, wait, then open the door to an unfamiliar young woman. "Yes?..." She is tall, pretty, with long hair, she could be transgender. She remains rooted in place, awestruck: "I just wanted to see if you are her? I saw the name on the front door? I can't believe that you are really her and anyone can just come up?" We part with a smile. I have no need to answer question marks that punctuate declarative sentences.

I return to my desk to look for the password that will allow me to access my blood test results so I can schedule an appointment for a bone density examination, but that appointment depends on another password, which will be handed over to me in person after undergoing the test. I remember that I need the district committee's approval in order to renew the prescription for a drug I take that prevents the recurrence of breast cancer, which infected me twice.

My genome disc has a password designed to avoid working your fingers to the bone and shows the entire picture threaded with the four letters of the DNA. I tried to outsmart the key to the codes' prison and use a single password for them all, but this proved impossible, "you cannot give a password that you have used on another website in the past – in the last six months – weak password, try another."

I try again. The different order of the letters of a name and a birth date, or my mother's name and date of birth, or half of my name and half my father's date of birth. I also try the different combinations according to the password's destination – banks, social security, ATM cards, health insurance, health care provider, my page on the city's website, computer support, cellular, phone, international calling provider, mail, Internet, Google, granddaughters' school, club membership, used bookstore membership, beauty salon membership, the *Kibbutz* publishing house, my own publishing House, the toy- store, emergency medical care. Passwords and user-names – the components of identity, the keys to doors which do not necessarily need to be opened.

Yael Dayan

Why must I be buried in passwords and rejected for every mistake whenever I want to order a product or a book? Accumulating mistakes indicates dementia and senility.

The doorbell rings again. I'm expecting a call from the Internet service provider, a delivery from the supermarket, and either a call from my daughter or more texts with photographs and good news. But the mail-carrier is at the door, holding an envelope that couldn't fit in the mailbox. It's another book that I ordered.

I am on the phone with the Internet technician, we are trying to fix the problem and I follow the instructions but we're not getting anywhere. All of the various technical support people assume that I am a senile old lady, with clumsy fingers and a dim memory and eyesight, that I type too slowly and cannot handle codes and passwords – why do I even bother them and what use could I possibly even have with machines that are too complicated for a woman's brain, much less a woman my age! They desperately inform me that a "senior repairman" will contact me tomorrow morning. I am overcome by joy and eager anticipation for the morning, but the day is not over yet. There is no reason, I think, that I cannot fix the problem the same way that I change a flat tire, or a light bulb in the halogen lamp. The same way I got my pilot's license for a single engine plane, the same way I edit documents on the computer, punctuating the Hebrew, or care for the infirm and disabled who are voiceless, the same way I proposed new bills and got them passed.

I manage to resuscitate the cellular phone; a simple matter of system settings. I got my revenge on the computer – deleting into archives all of the photos that someday I will get around to print and arrange in proper photo albums, as Dov diligently did, never looking down on the activity. I erased all of the temptations that appear on the computer and then I did the same for the phone and they are saved forever in some dark corner of a provider or a system or an operator, which has a password that needs to be changed every few months or "contact your local branch" or "you number in line is" or "your information is at risk" or "you won two million Euros" courtesy of Google, ATM, an inheritance from Ghana, a widow interested in finding partners for her million-dollar business ventures, the Economic Minister of East Timor, you won the lottery – just fill out this form and mail the processing fee, buy a coupon, buy a flat-screen, a 3D screen, a steak dinner, and tax-free day, gluten-free day, couples-massage spa day. I delete all of the messages for good and mark them as "spam" but the boundaries that I set are not secure enough and a few of them always manage to get through.

I get a text message from the contractor that was supposed to fix some water damage in my apartment informing me that he won't be coming; he apologizes and promises to be here tomorrow.

A text from one of the numerous chain stores notifies me that shirts/nuts/toys/cosmetics/ are now on sale for discount club members. *Steimatzky* the booksellers, have a new promotion deal – a free book and a tin of instant coffee, a hundred grams of almonds free, one of two or vice versa, 20%, 50%, 60% – weekend sales. L'Occitane/ facial cleanser/ teeth cleaner/ upholstery cleaner – the doorbell rings– do I want to buy a carpet for 30 NIS? The seller is an elderly Persian man, he looks at my floors and the

36

carpets that cover them – *kashan, bukhara, soumak,* more are rolled under the armoire so as not to completely cover the terracotta floors. He drinks a glass of water. "Does it look like I need another carpet?" I ask, and he tries his luck next door.

An email with a photograph of the grandchildren playing in the pool beside the rented villa, or wearing life-vests on board a boat sailing the river, on an endless white sandy beach, or swimming in the turquoise blue waters of the bay, and to think that I almost took out a gun and shot the computer…Which reminds me that I have a firearms license, a gun but no ammunition. I have an appointment at the Ministry of Interior next week to get their approval for the purchase of fifty 9mm bullets for the Beretta. Another day spent waiting, a password, security checks, parking, signing documents, the oxygen will probably run out by the time I finish waiting in line. "You have to come in person, we cannot authorize via courier nor can you give someone power of attorney to represent you." Perhaps this too is inscribed in my identity, not in my genome but in a communication and password hard drive. The very existence of the gun. Renewing its license. Hiding the weapon in one of my closets and the bullets in another, if I had them. Going through scenarios of break-ins, driving through the occupied territories at night, the death threats from settlers. Is it a pose, a facade I preserve? Nostalgia for something that I haven't experienced, the routine of renewing the license every three years – the shooting range, paying the fees, renewing a license for an object that I have no need for and receiving yet another piece of paper that will join the others stuffed in my overflowing wallet: credit cards, clothing store "gold" membership cards, my disability card, former *Knesset* member identification card (allowing free travel on public transportation), memberships for shoe stores and bookstores, ADI (National Transplant Member) card, a discount card for pet food (it's been years since I had a dog), sports equipment and gardening supply stores all over the country.

If by chance, I find myself in the upper Galilee in dire need of some fresh bulbs to plant, I can walk over to *Yodfat,* or to *Yagur* in spring, or to *Givat Brenner* when it's rose planting season, or the Jerusalem Hills if I move to the mountains in summer and decide to transplant my wilted geranium bushes that suffered from the humid climate of the seashore.

I return to the page every few hours. Plug in the oxygen, take a sip of water and and try to do some exercises: walking in place, arm stretches, breathing relaxation, abdominal work. Emily and I bake a vegetable pie, following a recipe recommended by the dietitian when I consulted with her to her due a lack of protein and my inability to tolerate, almost since birth, milk and dairy products. The pie is bland, it lacks the flakiness of a good crust and the richness of butter, and its ingredients, high in protein as they may be, fail to make a satisfying or appealing mix.

I lie down to rest and relax. I receive more photos from the Greek waters, the ferry, places that I have forgotten, and I revisit a memory of a trip on a yacht belonging to friends who lived in Athens and London and would sail together during the temperate seasons. The Greek Islands, with their mythology and ancient history, their sea, in Lefkada, where Sappho jumped to her death from the cliff – to the beach where

Yael Dayan

Aphrodite was found, swept away in the froth of the sea of Cyprus, to Ithaca, traditionally believed to be the birthplace of Odysseus, and to Meganisi (the big island) with its caves. The chef was busy preparing delicacies, the crew navigated, I switched back and forth from my bad Greek to excellent English and became as familiar with mythology and Greek poetry as I was with the stories of the Bible and the places where we envisioned our heroes.

Yael and Sisera beside the Kishon stream, Samson at the gates of Gaza, Elijah and the Prophets of the Baal on Mt. Carmel, the site of our third grade class trip from Nahalal. Thermopylae crossing and Corinth Canal left their mark when I read Plato's *The Symposium* and Euripides' *The Trojan Women*.

Agamemnon and Iphigenia, along with Laban and his daughters Rebecca and Leah, a Hebraic-Greek mosaic, with no God or faith, all allegory with more moral value on our side, or less so, in the Greek mythology.

I adopted a mixed Mediterranean home, from Tiresias to Job, in all shades of sea-blue and rocky expanses of land, olives, vines and figs. I am Durrell's *Justine*, in Cavafy's Alexandria, Rachel of the Kinneret and Leah [Goldberg] from Arnon St., the mumbling Pythia in Delphi, the Jewess from Theodorakis' ballad "Mauthausen" and Deborah by the Kishon stream.

I dance on the table at Aris San's Taverna "Arianna" in Yafo or Sirtaki on Stavros Beach in Crete. I see the photos of the grandchildren and am transported over fifty years earlier, to the era of a confused personality, sorting the grain from the straw that I once was.

The day is almost over, the air conditioning and the closed blinds have blurred the difference between night and day and my breathing is less laborious. The three lengthy conversations I conduct over the phone are cries for help, one is real and two are false alarms that merely seek attention.

All of them go straight to the locked room, guarding the privacy of others. I travel in my thoughts to the mythology of the Lethe river, crossing to its other side means that one is blessed with the gift of forgetting. An eternal loss of memory, erasing the sorrows of life. Do the dead on the other side of the river gather new memories? Do they forget the good things too or is it a curse related to the future possibility of a parallel world? The black hole, the hole that engulfs all matter, energy, light – diminishing until the point of singularity – infinite density and disappearance in a shrunken point of time on the axis of eternity.

And in the black hole there is a point of no return. Beyond it matter is not conserved. Not even its molecules. The law of conservation of mass, the transformation into another state – meaning cyclical, or total evaporation into nothing or transforming me into a turkey or a ladybug. At my age, old age, this is no source of consolation, but merely a matter for contemplation.

Chapter 5

The Sixties. A best-seller writer at 20 looking for identity-The world is in the palm of my hand, but am I Israeli? Jewish? Citizen of the World? Is going abroad breaking a siege or escaping a fairy tale?

I never travelled at breakneck speeds or allowed myself to get carried away by unrestrained passion. There were tail ends of fantasies, delights that stayed within limits and boundaries, I observed without losing myself, I kept a distance.

Even as a beautiful young woman, my long hair flowing, my lips bearing traces of sensuality, amusement and a healthy sense of self, I still remained rooted in a kind of defining circle. I never drank to intoxication, I didn't experiment with drugs, even when in the company of smokers and sniffers. I was never tempted to partake in exotic sexual encounters that I thought I would regret. I wasn't a prudish nun, nor was I frigid or lacking sexual curiosity, but the experiences I wanted to have with men never included threesomes or a group, and even with one partner I remained cautious, maybe apprehensive, always selective.

I had regrets, disappointments and my share of failures. But those belong to the woman I used to be. I do not know if the young Yael of that time, or the mature woman who later replaced her would do things similarly. In my youth I had my "red lines" but a decade later those lines changed or faded. Was it inconsistency? A shift in moral standards? I'll never know.

In every phase of my life I have been totally sure of myself, even when I was judgmental in the standards I set for myself and others, with the arrogant sensation that the world was in the palm of my hand. It was an arrogance accompanied by a passion for learning, understanding, containing. It was never condescending, but had the self-assurance of eventual success.

The late 1950s to 60s went by in a flash. I had a place in the front row of the world's mezzanine. During my IDF service I participated in the 1956 Sinai Campaign and in the Six-Day War as a first lieutenant in reserves. At a young age, I published my first book and it was very well-received; I met publishers, writers, poets. I was a sought- after lecturer. I was a soldier, a writer, the daughter of a general, a Sabra, native born Israeli, daughter of Sabras, an eloquent speaker. I went on voluntary lecture tours around the world, with only my expenses paid. The tours enabled me to gain an awareness of – and to participate in – the social movements that were burgeoning at the time. North and South America, West Africa Europe, Australia, New Zealand and The Far East– from Iran to Japan. I floated between worlds, cultures, continents touching down in Israel briefly and taking off again, disappearing for long stretches in order to work on a novel. Returning with a new book, a new love, and between stormy upheavals, I would stop to reflect, attempt to grasp my surroundings, I got lost, repeatedly, and then refocused. Literature. Poetry. Separating tone from rhythm, stage from decor, and the essential from the superfluous.

There were the cities that I loved and I had favorite streets, with "my" shops and cafes. I had a rented apartment in Athens, a favorite Greek island, my own unit at a London apartment suite, a particularly sweet editor in Paris and an agent that I admired in London. I hopped from government representatives–ministers and world Leaders –to the subversive groups and ideologies that I subsequently internalized, translating them into my language and absorbing them through my senses.

I came from a young state, that leaned towards the Labor movement, Socialism and welfare-state convictions. The form of Zionism I knew asked no questions, was secular and took the right that the Jews had to a homeland and human rights for granted. My roots were in my father's wars and mother's work with immigrant absorption, the worker's cooperative way of life in Nahalal and Degania, the poems of Rachel, Alterman and Shlonsky and the stories of Turgenev and Chekhov. I was schooled in them all, and then became familiar with Joan Baez and Bob Dylan, Tennessee Williams and Boris Pasternak, the Vietnam War and the Civil Rights Movement, Carson McCullers and Jack Kerouac, The Beatles, John F. Kennedy and Che Guevara, Hemingway and Albert Camus.

This is not a catalog, organized in alphabetical order, nor is it an index listed by order of importance. It's also not the boasting of a self-indulgent child, a display of the precious intellectual gems she has acquired. The list may be meaningless to whoever reads it or was born afterwards. This is not an inventory but a description of my foundation.

I came home often and then would quickly set off to Europe, the US, to the Far East and to an Africa that was just awakening from colonialism. For days I sat transfixed by the trials of Adolf Eichmann, began to gain a deeper understanding of what had transpired over there and the impact that over there had on our lives here. I understood– but was not caught up in– the fears of victimization, but was seized by the victory of the free spirit which continued to prevail in the aftermath of the War, a spirit of determination and the conviction of the triumph of justice.

There were changes in Israel as well. Our hemlines went up, we took to wearing fashionable knee high boots, we bravely embraced the bikini, were envious of the boyish Twiggy and Audrey Hepburn, and we scorned bourgeois conservatism, old fashioned norms, and expressions of inequality.

Transitions

I bought a small house in the artists' village Ein-Hod, and in addition to books I wrote articles and gave lectures. I belonged to a set that was "glamorous" and flashy, but I had no need to behave, be seen, or dress the same way the others did. Books were my entry ticket to the world, and after the Six–Day War I could add the badge of "parental merit", my father being an icon and a war hero. The world took a considerable degree of interest and pride in Israel post–1967. The new, controversial results of the occupation, land expropriation and annexation in the years after the Six–Day War did not stand out yet. What we considered to be temporary measures were hiding buds of evil and destruction.

I had numerous speaking engagements with American Jews. There was a consensus within the American Jewish community regarding the unwavering support for the Israeli government, the justness of the war, the struggle to absorb aliya immigrants and the need to consolidate a defense force. We were still a young country, the IDF and its commanders were the heroes of the Jewish people. Everyone loved seeing photographs of male and female soldiers bearing weapons and dancing the *hora* with the *kibbutz* children and an array of ethnic peoples in traditional garb.

Those were the fundraising posters. The punchline, the "clincher"–I cringed at the very sound of it, not to mention using it – was that "in Israel, we are giving our sweat and effort and the blood of our boys and girls, and all you have to do is pull out your checkbook." I believed that Israel needed to be a center for the Jews of the world, and that there were duties, I thought, such as absorbing immigrants, educating and promoting unity, cooperation and solidarity and accepting the different movements in Judaism, tasks that should be shared by Israel and the diaspora. However security, democracy or culture – those we shall cultivate and develop on our own.

I failed to see the warning signs of the occupation, and thought that we aimed to "exchange" the occupied territories for peace, and considered our extended hand for reconciliation to be a permanent and intrinsic part of our entity. Our Zionism. Our Judaic values.

From time to time I came down from the mezzanine to the front rows and even the basements. Some of my friends had been 'blacklisted" by Senator McCarthy, Hollywood directors and producers, writers and screenwriters were forced to relocate to Europe, London, Paris and Athens, because they couldn't find work and get funding in the US. I began to realize the limits of a democracy that used its mighty weight into order to "protect" the foundations via destructive paranoia. I was actively involved in the emerging discourse, in demonstrations, in feminist consciousness raising circles that devised plans and drafted manifestos, laws, demands and also diagnosed the feminine vulnerabilities and weaknesses and the hopes at breaking through barriers and overcoming the glass ceiling.

I was slow to realize that my backyard is years behind in shaping gender equality and fighting discrimination. Naively, we lacked a seismograph to foretell the disastrous earthquake about to shake our world from the inside.

In New York, I frequented the bars and salons, in the Village and at literary parties;

Yael Dayan

I found myself conversing with Truman Capote and Andy Warhol, having lunch at the Algonquin, where writers and publishers often met, with Thornton Wilder and the writers of the South, the greatest of all, Carson McCullers and Tennessee Williams.

I had other experiences as well, which were confusing to me as I lacked any trace of New York sophistication. A woman whom I deeply respected once misinterpreted my affection as an invitation for sex and I was beside myself with fear and embarrassment, as I blocked her hand when it began sliding between my legs. The woman was older and more experienced and most importantly, she had a good sense of humor, which I lacked during the incident. She apologized, I apologized, and under the cover of darkness and the cold weather, we retreated to our separate corners of the speeding yellow cab. She got off first and I continued to my hotel. After that night, I ran into her at various social events, but she never showed any signs that the encounter had left a memorable mark. Oops, a mistake! Next. On the other hand, I went through the event in my mind, trying to understand the meaning of the slight tremor that ran through me when I removed her hand.

I am not "name-dropping," I'm trying to revisit what constituted my entry point into other playing fields – a glimpse into the winding road of humanity, with its multitude of paths and richness of tastes.

Initially, I felt uneasy about revealing myself. Who are you? Who are you really? I had a need to create a complex identity, one that would be open to new friends that were communicating in manners of speech and physical contact that I had never encountered before.

What did we talk about? There was curiosity about Israel. Jews wondered whether we were observant and others asked about the degree of freedom that a democracy permits during times of war. There was a camaraderie of artists that oscilated between tradition and innovation, conservatism or permissive social norms, direct language and the responsibility that their country had in the events that were taking place in distant lands, including Israel.

I was easily persuaded to go in any direction that was put forth to me by someone whom I respected and admired.

I fell for superficiality and defended Israel with a patriotism that was foreign to my cynical counterparts.

I was like a wide-eyed student when they spoke about the injustices of racism, the infringement of the government on personal liberties, the responsibility that artists had for their countries of origin. The intellectuals and writers engaged with the failures of their own democratic government, fighting the violation of human rights and freedom of expression.

I was disconcerted by the blind admiration that feminist leaders showed towards Israel. They presumed that because we were a young country, patriotic, struggling on all fronts, we had also attained wondrous goals. The photographs of the female pioneers and soldiers were the main cause of this misconception, the images of women armed with hoes and weapons. I invested much thought, study and conducted long conversations in order to understand where we were and which direction we were heading, and clearly, in hindsight, I realize that the female characters in my books, even when they are strong, domineering, or manipulative, aren't actually independent and do not possess a real voice of their own. Even when they "have the upper hand" in the battle between the sexes, it's still a struggle, inharmonious. I myself was lacking in solidarity and empathy towards disadvantaged women. At the time, I wasn't concerned with the absence of representation that women had in government or other fields which were the sole domain of men, or by sexual harassment of female soldiers, employees and students, nor by economic inequality.

I found it hard to expand my concern to include things that were beyond my personal experience and elite status. I felt that I wasn't able to speak about the plight of the general public, about deeper insights that I had or socially oriented world-views. I began slowly formulating a way of looking at things that did not take anything for granted. I tried to understand women's needs and the limits of power, to discern what is unacceptable and the foundations that encourage various forms of discrimination: black and white, men and women, gay and straight, new immigrants and long-time residents, and in Israel, religious and secular too.

I was a twenty-three year old straight woman, the daughter of Ashkenazi parents, born and raised in Israel, secular as can be, and I needed to get my heart and my head in order. To juxtapose feelings and thoughts. I didn't consider myself to be a good example, because I thought I was in control. I wasn't harassed, but rather was the one tempting and flirting. Julliard Publishers in France, who published Christiane Rochefort, Marguerite Duras and my own book along with that of Francoise Sagan were not pushing any of us aside to accommodate male writers. As a writer I faced no gender competition. My reigning queen of new insight was Simone De Beauvoir and I had "A Room Of My Own."[9]

I don't know what came first – my familiarity with the poetry of Cavafy or André Gide's *The Immoralist*, or my close friendship with Yossi Stern. [10] In any case, I became naturally involved in gay and lesbian rights, both culturally and socially.

Initially, perhaps there was some childish curiosity on my part, but that quickly made way for acceptance and understanding, and to this day I believe that nothing compares to the friendship between a woman – or a young woman– and a homosexual man, an artist, in love, betrayed, forgiving, laughing, weeping, folded in an embrace with a different kind of love, devoid of tension.

It's an opportunity for a shared cultural journey, to delve deep into art, literature, poetry, into the pleasures of love, true friendship without sex.

Yossi and I painted Jerusalem in bold colors – new to me. We danced ourselves dizzy at 'The Artist's House,' doing everything from the pasodoble to refined waltzes, we were always the last couple on the dance floor. We enjoyed the thick, spicy goulash soup at Fink's restaurant and with utmost discretion, Yossi would delicately hint when

9 See Virginia Woolf, "A Room of One's Own" (1929).
10 An Israeli figurative painter.

I needed to clear the way for his beloved partner. Oftentimes we simply wandered the alleys that led to his house in Nachlaot.

I tried to learn from the greats during that decade. The signs of the revolution were budding everywhere. The old world order had been shaken. There was a sense of liberation in the air, of rebellion. The wind had blown from the flower children and their anti-war protests, Elvis Presley, the attitude towards the Cold War, Kennedy's "Ich bin ein Berliner," *The Feminine Mystique* by Betty Friedan, who, when we met, captured my imagination and impressed me with her courage and boldness. I travelled the world but the social and cultural insights and convictions I gained were mainly in the US. I followed Kennedy, the Civil Rights Movement, the struggles of the minorities, Vietnam and the Cold War. I tried to shape my worldview with no preparation from home, or so I thought. Israel was ten years old when I completed my service in the IDF. I knew the *Israeli Declaration of Independence* by heart and naively believed that those would be our ten commandments for generations to come:

"...ensure complete equality of social and political rights to all its inhabitants irrespective of religion, race or sex; it will guarantee freedom of religion, conscience, language, education and culture…"

This is how I was raised. My grandparents vigilantly guarded these principles. They took care to always consider others, to remain modest. They were secular – Grandmother Rachel made a point of it– and democratic in their ideology, and way of life, with firm certainty and a full awareness of the alternatives.

The struggles that went on all over the world seemed unrelated to Israel. It was inconceivable that hatred on the basis of sexual orientation, discrimination against women, racism, religious coercion, or a refusal of peace could ever exist here. Not here, not among us, I thought. It cannot be. I didn't know much about what was happening beyond the circle of Nahalal and the elitist schools where I was raised. The military service was embedded with superficial patriotic slogans. We were proud, courageous and obedient, answering the call of duty. At seventeen I did not even try to look deeper into the axiomatic truths, the male domination of the entire scene, individual needs or preferences. I was protected by a liberal, egalitarian, rational world. Everything I knew about violence, discrimination and fanaticism came from books and was not present in my immediate surroundings.

A narrow world coupled with a broad autodidactic education was a sure recipe for disaster. Rewarding and exciting self-directed learning was fused with immature perceptions and generalizations. There were provocations and superficial rebellion on my part, along with a compulsive hunger to comprehend, to perceive, to be completely independent and at the same time resist releasing whoever came too close.

I was ready to write my first book, shying away from everything familiar and the comforts of home. I wrote in solitude, in a friend's house in Brittany, France, in a small apartment in Athens, in an apartment-hotel in London. Those were the early 1960s and they brought about a sharpening of the senses and reassessment of values. I was a student of the chapter in human rights; getting to know "the other." Harlem, the South, gospel and protest music and a tour of Africa – from Soweto in Johannesburg with a Jewish doctor who devoted her life to the struggle of black people in her country, to the dishearteningly corrupt palaces in Liberia and Congo, and the voodoo ceremonies in incense-filled caves and the echo of the drums in the suburbs of Bahia and watching thrilling soccer games with Pelé at the Maracanã in Rio de Janeiro. I memorized the poems on "the love that dare not speak its name, "Rimbaud, Verlaine, Oscar Wilde and Byron, and I made friends with human rights protesters. I saw young girls weaving carpets in Isfahan, tying the colorful threads with small hands and burying their childhoods in the dark alleyways as enslaved women. Before I turned twenty-three years old, I watched as widowed women were set on fire on the rafts in the Ganges River and the odors, the tastes and the questions stayed with me long afterwards, fierce and disturbing. I was beginning to comprehend painful realities, and the understanding gave rise to my commitment to shake up and rewrite the old agendas.

My own world seemed so protective and controlled. The small country had no routes leading out of it by land , you could only go westward towards the sea or upwards, taking to the air. It had a rich and multi-layered history and archaeology, was busy working out its identity, and had successfully revived a language but remained undecided as to what moral code it should follow.

What I found in the world outside was stirring and enrapturing. It was new in magnitude and intensity, in the endless possibilities and the ways you could navigate among the multiple choices.

Going abroad was a luxury, an expensive indulgence that enriched the mind. In North America and the Europe that I was familiar with, all the struggles pertained to identity, equality and difference; they were about social disparities and achievements in science, research, art, in limitless opportunities, breakthroughs and experiences that went beyond what was normative and safe –provoking moral issues both positive and negative.

The Vietnam War was far from home and from the discourse of most of the people I knew. My Jewish audiences were mostly Democrats, and Israel's 'narrow waistline' was more of a concern to them than the night raids on the Viet-Cong or the very issue of the violent involvement that was growing more and more complicated on the other side of the world.

I was well aware of our conflict with the Arab world surrounding us. I thought, in good faith, that eventually it would be solved, that it had to be solved. I took Zionism to literally mean the establishment of a people and a country, a national home. A struggle for the quality of matters within the borders, rather than an expansion of them. I never felt threatened.

I harbored no hatred of Arabs, no fear of an "enemy" nor did I have any aspirations to conquer or seize control of anything that was not mine–neither did my family. The Bible, its history and geography were a wellspring of language, poetry and a measure of morality, rather than a source of religious faith. The Holy Scripture didn't instill the fear of God within me, or a commitment to follow religious decrees or prohibitions. I didn't expect the good lord to fulfill his promise to the chosen people, my people had vanished over the 2000 years of Diaspora and the smoke rising from the gas chambers at Bergen-Belsen. I loved the stories, the proverbs and the visions of the prophets, but didn't consider myself to be an extension of the 'People of Israel' in the Promised Land, or hold a grudge or wish to retaliate against the people of Amalek. I saw myself as an Israeli residing within the internationally accepted borders of my country. And yes, I belonged to an ancient culture, heritage and most importantly, I partook in the revival of an ancient language with the Zionist movement and the establishment of the Hebrew-speaking democratic state.

I was born as the Second World War broke out in Europe. My father's brother, Zorik, my beloved uncle, was killed in the War of Independence.

He was the first person that I knew and loved who died. I was enlisted during The Sinai Operation 1956. I never questioned or sought to justify our military operations. I subsequently served as an officer in the reserves during the 1967 Six–Day War where I fell in love with Dov – my future husband and was swept up in the tumultuous spirit of victory and hope. I covered my young children protectively during the Yom Kippur War in 1973 and then put on the soldier's uniform again, perplexed, completely dependent on my husband Dov, his maturity and experience guided my attempts to understand, as he promised that it would be the last war.

I was brought up in a military family; the 'red phone' hotline was a fixture at my parents' bedside table and military jargon and slang were an inherent part of my life. After completing my IDF service, I spent long periods abroad when I was in between books, but I always came home, to the warmth and love of my family, to the books, newspapers and my daily life as a civilian, which was a cross between a bohemian and a bourgeois suburban lifestyle.

As I grew older, I realized that 'daily life as a civilian' occurred during cease fires, that peace is possible only if genuinely desired, that there is profit to be made even from wars that are always won, that the phrase "peace at the price of painful concessions" is empty and devoid of meaning and intent, that it is easier to frighten with the horrors of war than to motivate people to make compromises for peace.

Perhaps not everything is coordinated in a single system of a mind. Maybe the brain that did the developing, inventing and improving , cannot control the connection of neurons erupting and directing all stimuli towards the destructive red button and neutralizing every other option. Man, in his weakness or might, releases scentless, tasteless gas, bacteria, toxic particles to devour populations invisible to the eye without blood, killing children. It's a choice, taking cover under the guise of 'no alternative'.

The second half of the previous century was the era of great wars, ones that pitted good against evil, and there were victories that promised a better world. Systems were put in place to balance and check, to create order, facilitate communication and prevent violations of the common human code of conduct.

And the battle was necessary in our parts too; it was just, it defended us and shaped our identity. When I was a girl, a teenager and a young woman, I accepted the struggle as the means to attain the sublime goal we had dreamed of. Yet in the past decades a widening chasm has appeared, and choice now belongs to the strong, not the just. And ever since, our conscience cannot be clear and justice has no foothold, and there is no cover for the shame of the victorious. It has been more than four decades since I admired a military uniform, rank or medal. My uniform, my father's, Dov's and those of our friends, living or dead. I have distinguished between the blood- stained ones, even the ones soaked with the blood of enemies, that have been respectful on the road to the nation's survival and flourishing, and between those that were wrinkled with the doubts of the multitudes that were pledging allegiance to false flags, chasing imperious honors and chiming treacherous bells.

When did you change? When did the girl clad in khaki army-fatigues become a woman in black? You used to be the poster child for the IDF. When your father was a Major General, he would take you on jeep excursions to the wadis and craters before there was even a proper road to Eilat and you went searching for flint stone arrowheads, amongst the jerboas and the unfamiliar desert birds. Your learned how to read a map and spot animal tracks, you soaked up the visionary freedom songs about the land in olden times, desert oases and waterways. The borders, the enemy, danger – none it was even mentioned. You, your father and your people had not emerged victorious with the bounty of war, nor were you occupiers. You saw yourself as a natural part of the land. Every summer you went to camp, hard at work picking apples at Neot Mordechai or laboriously clearing stones in Sde-Boker, first loves, disappointments, the new curves of a young woman late to develop, stolen fruit and exhilarating volumes of poetry. Every fallen soldier was sanctified and the army uniform was a pure sign of honor, rank – and had an attractive appeal. You signed up for this shade of military green and you excelled as an officer, subjects that you dealt with in your first book – a sense of belonging, a mission, innocence and faith.

Under the *chuppah,* the bridal canopy, you wore white and Dov was in uniform, Ariel Sharon, the best man, was Major-General and your father was Minister of Defense at the time and the Chief Military Rabbi who brought you together in holy matrimony, was starting to show the first signs of the twisted messianism that would later completely take over.

***

We endured the war, another 'last war.' With the hopeful sensation that peace was bound to come, I made us a home and got pregnant. I dismissed Dov's hesitation and apprehensiveness as part of the excessive concern he had for his independence. We both knew our way around the world. Dov was almost twenty years my senior, he had experienced loss, battle, dashed hopes and plans that had gone awry, and now finally, he allowed himself a small measure of tranquility. I felt satisfied, peaceful, and enjoyed a new-found affection towards my parents – even if it was towards each one individually. Hand in hand we waited, filled with anxiety and hope, for the event that was about to bring about a profound change we could not foresee.

Dan, our firstborn, was born a year and a half after the war.

I tried to erase the moment of his birth from my memory. We didn't know the gender of the baby beforehand. I went through labor, endured all the pain, and finally heard the blessed sound, a faint bleating of a baby breathing on its own, and through the tears that were pouring down on my face, the midwife delivered the news:

"*Mazal tov*, we have another soldier!" More tears and chills ran through me, and the midwife soothed me: "don't cry, everything is alright, I swear…"

Dov and I traded our military uniforms for the thrilling new blanket of parenthood.

A child borne of our love to share, and the entirely new, intense affection for the small being that suckled at my breast enthusiastically, whom I caressed with caution and a gentleness I never felt before. The sensation pushed aside the entire content of my world and left no room for anything apart from his tiny perfect head, the wonder of creation in his movements, the grip of his fingers and the sound of his cries, his murmurings and the expression on his face as it rested on Dov's shoulder when his father lulled him to sleep with the pleasant sound of his voice.

Dov accepted a position as a military attaché in Paris, and our family soon represented the IDF in suits and formal attire. Dan was the centre of our lives, we learned by trial and error and I broke all of the rules in the book. The child was spoiled, he lacked boundaries and no need of his went unmet for long. We would race each other to see who would be first to pick him up whenever he cried or stumbled. He was closely watched and admired. Dov filmed and recorded and wrote to him, his room was piled with unnecessary toys, and he developed quickly – talking and walking at an early age. I cannot help but burst into tears whenever I recall the first time that he said "Ima" and "Aba." Unsurprisingly, he didn't want to share our love with his sister, who was born when he was two.

After a series of seemingly singular events like war and love, we returned to Israel to our permanent home. It was equipped with a nursery and a kitchen that had been selected according to my taste, and in the back of the apartment there was a desk, which tested my devotion to the children every day, for it pitted them against my desire to devote time to writing. My half a day of freedom when they were in kindergarten and preschool clarified the fact that in effect, the two did not conflict. In the midst of my apprenticeship in a tedious culinary cycle, which my children didn't budge from: meatballs-mashed potatoes-schnitzel-French-Fries-pasta-dessert, and with Dov's support and encouragement, I wrote another novel.

Dov either evaded the children's questions about his parents altogether or gave them brief answers. My parents had plenty of grandchildren, and when my father remarried, his new wife's grandchildren joined the magical garden in Tzahala , and I will never know if we managed to compensate for the children's loss of their grandparents, David and Rachel, who died in the death march from Auschwitz during the final months of WWII.

Transitions

I wasn't an anxious mother, but undoubtedly, working from home when the children were young, picking them up them from kindergarten and school, the interest and preoccupation with their homework and school activities, the frequent nature hikes, the beach, travelling abroad when possible, with Dov and without him, all cushioned my life, I gave them a solid layer of security, a suburban routine that protected them and satisfied myself.

We left for Paris as newlyweds, after the acclaimed victory of the Six Day War. We were absent during the following four years and weren't involved on a daily basis nor were we aware of the tremendous changes that began to occur. The possibility of peace with Egypt, the redefinition of the borders in the areas that were occupied and a growing sentiment within a country that became enamored with the concept of a greater Israel – from the sea to the river Jordan. My parents divorced when we were in Paris and our children, Dan and Racheli were born.

A short time after we returned from Paris, the Yom Kippur War broke out.

Another war. This time I am a mother, but I still don a uniform when called up to serve. The last in a line of life-or-death wars, a victory and at the same time a breaking point, in hindsight, an inevitable war on the road to peace.

We have been very strong ever since the war; our warehouses overflow, heaven and earth belong to us, and had the smoke risen and clouded everything over or had the land been scorched and ceased to exist, it would be because we remain ravenous, we were never satiated and we never took off the uniform to put on civilian clothing. We never cast off the Yellow Star, sending it to the infirmary to forever be a remnant of the past, but instead we wanted to wave it like a flag, like a pillar of fire that lead to property that was not our own, as a justification for all of the choices we made. For the deaths of children. Our children, the victims of terror and terrorist shooting attacks, the children that are all shahids, led on the via dolorosa that their fathers have paved, children caught in the crossfire, or playing in the wrong place, or crossing the fence, or throwing stones…always throwing stones.

Some to the Moloch and others fettered in preparation for sacrifice.

In 'wars of choice' there is no component of good and bad, or the inevitable, a force majeure, right and wrong. We choose. We separate one blood from another, one color from another, believers and infidels, in the name of the Lord who chose us above all other nations. Forever avenging the yellow star.

You cannot live with that. You cannot die for it either.

My father died before the Lebanon War and Dov was in uniform and reported for duty and in Sabra and Shatila children were slaughtered. I went to the square, dressed in black.

Ever since, as a mother and a grandmother, I count the children, the limits of their lives and the soft horror of their deaths.

Summer is coming to an end. I am a seventy-four-year-old grandmother, a retired civil servant, the widow of a high-ranking IDF officer, living off of pension plans, and my entire body begins shaking when I see the pictures from the Syrian village of

Yael Dayan

Zamalka. Pictures of chemical slaughter, the bodies of children marked by numbers, a two month baby girl, number fourteen, not identified by name. A five year old boy, number thirty.

The images of the children's bodies in Syria shrouded in white, silent, looking like they were sleeping on their backs, their arms crossed in a frozen gesture. You are beside yourself with pain which defies all words and meaning. Can you really contain the pain of the victims according to the nature of the perpetrators; do you think that the identity of the hangman delineates the suffering of the hanged?

Someone put them in a line; the first ones are on one side and all of the legs, limp and lifeless, on the other. You are frightened. Borrowed memories from Dov rise up like a thick cloud, the Death March, Dov's nightmares as he tries to dig up the body of Ya'akov, his brother, buried in the snow that is rapidly piling up.

To the northeast, a storm of blood is raging between disputing brothers. Every day and every night, children die in fires and shootings and bombings, children who will not grow up, not even in order to hate and avenge the disfiguring phosphorous that attacked them. Forty years ago, the spring earth crumbled and graves gaped open to receive the bodies of the children slaughtered in *Ma'alot*. [11] Your father's lone eye shone with tears as he supported a man who was crying out at the funeral of his son murdered in *Avivim*. [12]

There is no logic to the agitation and turmoil that I experience when confronted with the death of children. Is it that they are innocent? That their lives still haven't bloomed?

That they are weak and defenseless, that the balance of power and evil, exploitation and cruelty cannot include them? Inside of me, within the warmth of my navel and the breath of my life, the murdered child, the severed baby, the stabbed little girl – they are the essence of the loss of humanity, the end of morality and the defeat of existence.

My admiration for my daughter increases; she is a Pediatrician in the PICU at the Wolfson Hospital [13], member of Save A Child's Heart saving the damaged hearts and lives of thousands of babies and children, mostly Palestinians from the Occupied Territories and Africa, including children from Syria and Iraq.

In my frustration, I momentarily become Hagar:

> "And she went, and sat her down over against him a good way off
> as it were a bowshot: for she said, Let me not see the death
> of the child. [14]"

For a moment and never more. To know and look away is to participate.

I do not give up. I am familiar with indifference, the shrugging of shoulders, the

---

11 An Israeli town where children were massacred.
12 An Israeli town where children were massacred
13 Pediatric Intensive Care Unit in Wolfson Hospital
14 Genesis 21:16

search for the guilty party, the hesitation, the "but" and "that's the way it is." I am also well acquainted with the debilitating feeling that grips me when I see babies being killed twice, five times, and when they are buried other babies are sought out and killed, I gather my bearings, shake myself off and prepare to resume the struggle.

Chapter 6

When did I change from a Girl in Khaki to a Woman in Black?
Wars of Choice?

Right now, in this deceptively versatile city, people are waiting on two different lines. One is a group of mothers with babies and young children, waiting to receive "two drops," an immunization for the prevention of polio – a disease that was supposedly eradicated. The other is a line of adults, fighting to keep their places as they wait to receive their gas mask kits. Two drops of a live virus – attenuated. There have been no cases of polio for twenty-five years, and we thought that the disease had been wiped out, but when it returned – two drops. The damage to the nervous system causes paralysis and in some cases death by cardiac arrest. Vaccinations have made the disease rare, but now the virus has been detected in sewage from the southern and central parts of the country, and the vaccine is necessary in order to prevent the threat of disease in the population at large. There is a long line of impatient mothers at the *Tipat Halav* public health clinic for babies and children, including ones that do not want their children to be vaccinated, alongside refugee children from Africa, babies and children waiting in the heat of summer – and preparations are also underway for the start of the new school year and the traditional apple dipped in honey, which marks Rosh Hashana.

At the same time, there is a line for gas masks. Due to the rows of the dead shrouded in white in the suburbs of Damascus, due to fear, due to the unknown, which is not mystical, an act of magic, or a blow delivered by god, but an act of man.

Even our fears, protecting our children and the responsibility towards others, have different levels to them. The line for the masks is longer because clearly, there will not be enough of that kind of protection for everyone, so it's first come, first served.

The last time there were long lines for the cardboard gas mask kits was during the Gulf War in 1991. I was in uniform, serving in the IDF Spokesperson's Unit. The masks remained in the brown boxes but Dov reluctantly sat in the sealed room whenever the sirens sounded. My son Dan and his girlfriend anxiously moved from place to place, my daughter Racheli was in the army and I wasn't worried about her. I walked the streets of the city, which was practically empty, I climbed up onto rooftops in order to brief the foreign journalists who wanted to see the missile paths of the "Scuds" and the "Patriots." I visited sites that had been left unlocked with a kind of fatalistic indifference, and occasionally dropped in on friends too. My colleagues and I produced a "Daily Report" in English for the IDF Spokesperson, which included a list of chemical and biological weapons; the information had to be accurate – before the advent of Wikipedia. Safety instructions. Moral arguments. Photographs of missile strikes. A letter-coded map dividing the country into different zones. I drove through Zones B and G, and travelled to Zone C, nodding at the people who, fearing for their lives, decided to leave Tel Aviv for the safety of more remote areas.

I didn't have much faith in the wet rags we were told to put underneath the door frames in the sealed rooms, and I also freed Dov from the uncomfortable nightmare of putting on the gasmask every time an alarm sounded. Instead, we stood together in front of the large window that faced west in our Ramat Aviv apartment, watching the city the same way we once watched fireworks with the children at Disneyworld in Orlando. Every once in a while we saw the "Patriot" missiles launching, their bright glow lining the sky. The neighbors stayed in the safety room on our floor, which was neither sealed or secured, but to me the situation simply wasn't threatening. The atmosphere on the streets at night was pleasantly bizarre. The difference between "real" wars, wars of choice and wars of necessity, could clearly be sensed, and the restraint that Israel showed by not responding was convincing.

In the summer of 2013, the leaders in Israel were disappointed in the American rejection of an attack, which they demanded and eagerly anticipated. An infatuation with wars of choice, even when we have failed at them. We have our red lines that have nothing to do with the nature of the weaponry or the type of conflict. It is a red line that is drawn in accordance with the sentiment of victimhood that has been ingrained within us, and is certainly intensified with the mention of nerve gas. The very threat upon us, be it real or hypothetical, inflames the glands of memory, which call for an immediate, full- blown reaction. In the name of "never again" we will support an attack or instigate one under the pretext that the risk is always, in the final analysis, our own. It is not fear driving decision makers, it's evil, a sense of revenge and a blinding excess of power.

In the meantime, I am at home. I have not been vaccinated for polio and I don't have a gas mask; the first had yet to be invented when I was a child and I gave my mask to Emily, who isn't eligible to receive one at the distribution center that the Home Front Command set up, and I couldn't even find one to purchase for her.

When the sirens sounded in Tel Aviv, I was hospitalized in the Geriatric Rehabilitation Center, having suffered multiple fractures in my back and hip. Every movement involved excruciating pain, and my legs could not carry me. When the siren sounded, the nurses directed patients who were mobile towards the stairwell, but and I stayed put, watching the television that hung over my narrow bed, counting the minutes or the hours that separated one pill or shot of painkillers from another, not taking much interest in the sirens.

My mother was also resting in her bed during the attacks and we spoke over the telephone. She was flooded with memories of different bombings.

About seventy years earlier, Tel Aviv had been bombed from the air. I was two years old, a neighbor was taking care of me while my mother volunteered at Hadassah[15] in Tel Aviv. My father was in a British jail in Acre. After treating the wounded who were rushed to the hospital, my mother hurried home to find much of it destroyed while I was still sitting in my crib, without a scratch on me.

The story was added to our family's collection of miraculous tales, only my sandals were said to have been lost in the commotion.

Years later my mother showed me a letter that she had written to my father in jail, describing that day.

September 10, 1940

My Darling,

Where shall I begin. You once wrote that you envisioned us amongst bombs and ruins...and it came true. I am still in a state of shock. Perhaps I will start at the beginning. You already know that I have began working at the trauma center at Hadassah. On Monday, meaning yesterday, I put Yulik down for her nap at one thirty p.m. and went to work until evening. Zipporah was the only one home; she was out in the yard doing the laundry. We were the only two volunteers at Hadassah and we were complaining that there was nothing for us to do, and an hour later we heard a kind of earthquake, the windows rattled, I thought that the building was collapsing. We didn't even have time to think before the wounded began arriving, dozens of them. We worked frantically, and my darling, you need not be ashamed of me. We saw humans crushed beyond recognition.

We saw children split in half, babies without arms and legs, people drawing their final breaths, heads split open, hunks of flesh, and everything passed through my room. I suppose that I lost the capacity for emotion. I worked quietly, I went up to the operating room, I dressed wounds, I looked at everyone and I kept strangers out, and while working for hours I knew that Yulik was in the area that had been bombed, but I didn't think of that. I realized

15 Hadassah Women's Zionist Organisation, founded in 1912, is a women's volunteer group devised to meet health needs in Israel.

that I was on duty and whispered "Yulik" to myself in order to gain strength. I met an English officer in the hallway who was carrying a child about her age, covered in dust. I went over to take the baby and he said: "It's no use, he's dead," and I kept thinking that maybe it was Yulik and I hadn't recognized her, but nevertheless I went on in the same manner until eight p.m. and when the rooms were finally empty and everyone had been transferred to the hospital...I asked if I could find out where my daughter was. Of course, they immediately permitted me to do so, and they probably already knew what had happened because two nurses accompanied me home. The way home was filled with destruction and ruin, the streets covered in glass from the shattered shop windows, houses were destroyed on Bugrashov st., the shacks had burned down and it was dark outside. I reached home and my heart sank, the frame was the only thing that remained. Everything was destroyed, the fences, the hedge, the closets, cupboards, there were giant holes in the walls, and inside was an enormous avalanche. I called for Yulik and she was not there. At first I couldn't believe that she was alright. I thought that they were deceiving me and that something had happened to her and they were hiding it from me.

But it turned out that Reuma had taken her to a friend's to eat because it was impossible to stay in the house. I ran like a madwoman to find her and I will never forget the moment we met. All of the tension and my composure melted away and I actually cried when she embraced me and called out, Mommy. And the first thing that she said was that Daddy Moshe will come and take her and Mommy on a trip. She must've understood something, because she hugged me tight and kissed me. My darling, can you understand the hell that I endured yesterday, what it's like to see children like Yulik with no faces, hands, crushed? It was only when I held Yulik in my arms, safe and sound, that the day's horrors rose up before me. And then I found out what had happened to Yulik. She was sleeping, Zipporah was out in the yard doing laundry, the bomb fell about seven meters away from the house and from Zipporah, who was saved because she immediately fell to the ground. After the bomb exploded, Zipporah shouted the girl, the girl, and the house was dark with dust and smoke. They found Yulik sitting on the couch and crying, covered in plaster and dust and everything around her was shattered and destroyed, she was only thing that remained intact in the entire room. The shrapnel even reached the inner wall, which was full of giant holes. My darling, do you realize the miracle that occurred and can you appreciate what happened? Our poor Yulik, and I knew nothing of it, and even if I did I wouldn't have left the station, and I thought how absurd it was that you are in prison now and we are on our own...

Your father was in Jerusalem that day, we tried to notify him that we were safe but we couldn't get through and naturally, they were awake all night worrying because the lists of the dead had not been released. We couldn't sleep at all last night. First of all, I slept with Reuma and Yulik in the same bed and all through the night I could see severed hands, sterile bottles, again and again until I thought I'd burst, I thought I was becoming a complete wreck and would be done for because I was so nervous. In any case, I didn't sleep a wink and I decided to get Yulik to Jerusalem as soon as possible...In the morning I went to Hadassah and asked for permission to leave, and on our way to the Egged bus station, we met my parents and your father there, who had already come down from Jerusalem to find out what had happened to us. mother had tears in her eyes when she saw Yulik crying out in joy...My love, I desperately need a broad shoulder to lean on right now, my love. And to hold me. But apparently, despite everything, my spirit has not been broken and I look forward to resuming my work. My darling, reality is so difficult and bitter. I don't think I have the strength to laugh anymore, except when I am with Yulik. How will I leave her, I do not know, my love. All kinds of people have telephoned to give me their blessings and some have come to see Yulik. All of our clothes are now filled with holes, a piece of shrapnel is even lodged in Yulik's stroller. We searched up and down and finally found Yulik's sandals, but in the meantime she got new shoes...the scene at the house is awful....have you been worried or did you know nothing of this? I will most certainly be done in another week and of course, I have no idea what I will do afterwards, if I stay alive, according to the leaflets dropped in the Arab villages, it seems that they want to annihilate Tel Aviv...

There were no red lines during "that war" and there was certainly no one around to delineate them. A red line separates between bearable and unbearable evil, the latter being asymmetrical, of a different order, prohibited. On one side of the red line lies murder, rape, clubbing someone to death, striking them with arrows or targeted missiles and mass destruction with "conventional" warheads, but what lies on the other? Who determines these lines, and who in our world hasn't crossed them? You cannot use the weapons that you are allowed to produce and store – when can you use them? What about the atomic bombing of Hiroshima and Nagasaki which ended the war? Napalm, cluster bombs and anthrax powder, who is the overseer and who determines the moral norms or gages the balance of power? Does saving lives permit the use of mustard gas?

Whomever you rise up to kill is going to use everything at their disposal, and then the doors to the arsenals of weapons of mass destruction swing open, odorless gases evaporating in the air, or bacteria spreading in the water, infecting upon contact. We live with the permanent notion that people wake up and go to bed with the intent to wipe us out, and surely, as we have stated," We will not be the first to use that kind of weaponry." Nuclear ambiguity. Void of meaning.

The red line prohibiting the use of chemical or biological weapons is not clear to me, but I can feel it. It's as if an alien virus is threatening to take control of a familiar program that includes guns and bombs, missiles and warheads, and as if within the horror of the killing of innocent people that is not done in self-defense and real time, there are other lines in different colors, which are not part of our palate. Maybe it's because of the silence. Maybe blood and crushing limbs has something comprehensible and controlled about it, whereas the slack faces with their eyes closed belong to an unattainable ghost world, beyond the red line. Had I studied chemistry...science...medicine...had I understood, even then I would've still left the laboratory to protest, to catch the devil that was released and discover that he is within us after all and his dance of death feeds on the fire of perpetual, never ending victimhood.

My mother's grandfather, "Grandpa Dov," a grave, tall, slightly intimidating man, was a chemist. He studied at the Sorbonne and came to Palestine full of ideas that he wanted to implement. He was at the "Arazim (Cedar) Valley" for a period of time – in Motza. The cedar trees were cypresses and the trees that beckoned him were olive trees. He manufactured soap from olive oil, but lacked ample funding for a proper production line and he moved around a great deal. He separated from his wife – Great-Grandma Pnina, who was a Maternity nurse at Hadassah in Tel Aviv and lived with a roommate in a rented apartment – eventually settling in Haifa.

He continued to work in his field, producing fleet, a pesticide for mosquitoes and flies. My mother remembers the buckets of olives in Motza and liquid fleet in the bathtub in Haifa that was poured into old wine bottles and sold as a filler for the "flee-tiya," the cannister with a handle that compressed the liquid so it came out as a light spray that did indeed kill mosquitoes and was widely used, I remember it from Nahalal. But Grandpa Dov couldn't find the happiness and fulfillment that he was looking for there either. He had occasional financial backers to support his experiments, and taught chemistry at a high school in Haifa.

The pesticide industry continued to develop, eventually producing the tasteless and odorless compounds that kill children as well.

You take comfort in the fact that there are adamant pursuers of peace among the chemists and physicists that have received Nobel and Israel Prizes. They possess knowledge, insight and deep feeling and they will surely manage to put an end to the need to implement destructive knowledge. Does the very existence of a radical violent option eradicate the more moderate possibilities of discourse and discussion?

Transitions

In hindsight, the efforts that you and your friends made for peace seem small and pathetic. Your sensitivity was touching and the glimmers of hope never faded even when the fire had gone out and the sky turned dark. A physical sensation pulses through your body, and it is entirely helpless when faced with the children, the smoke, the sound of the explosions, the rolling thunder, destroying all good tidings, the soldiers coming towards me, rejoicing in a battle of Mars.

You do not give up and you will not dismiss the terror, banishing it to the horizon, instead, you drag your feet to a another protest march or meeting, another opportunity, you collect newspaper clippings describing the injustices or offering new, exciting avenues you have yet to discover.

The most significant of those efforts were the meetings with senior members of the Palestinian Authority. The small Israeli group was comprised of prominent writers, three Israel Award-winning scientists, two economists and me. The meetings fostered a sense of trust and honesty; all emotions were taken into account, all past initiatives and actions. After careful consideration of the controversial issues, there was a sense of sad optimism when the utter lack of symmetry became clear. We agreed on the solutions and practical implementations. However the Palestinians were part of the Authority, were closely associated with the President and represented their people. On the other hand, we were just a handful of people speaking on behalf of a sane, wise and powerless minority. Unable to afford despair, unable to tolerate the checkpoints, the uprooting of olive trees and the random shooting of kids throwing stones. Painfully so.

Ashamed of my beloved country that has sustained the occupation for decades—bolstered by the incited masses that are bound by hysteria and fear.

Extremist leadership that may harbor the buds of Fascism. I am frightened.

Chapter 7

I don't want to cross the finish line, just to get close. The Acarina were defeated and the flowers recovered.

It is *Rosh Hashanah* and the hyacinths are starting to bloom. You can feel the dry evening chill in the mountains, but there is still no sign of autumn in Tel Aviv, and my lung capacity declines in the thick humid heat; it has reached the point where I have to use the oxygen generator at home too. I find myself short of breath whenever I rush, even if it's just to answer the phone, and my body immediately reacts when I get emotional or upset; my lungs don't release enough oxygen into the bloodstream, the saturation levels fall and my breath trembles. I need to stop and take deep gulps of air for a good few minutes, sighing heavily on the exhales, before I can regain my composure.

President Obama just announced that war will not break out next week, to the great disappointment of its proponents. Anxiety has been dispelled, but soon the lines in the grocery stores start to grow long as people begin to maniacally stock up for the holidays. The air is abuzz with questions – who will attend, who will host the holiday meal and what shall we cook – as if there was ever any intention of varying the usual menu of fish and chicken soup with kneidlach. Seventy years of eating the same holiday meal has caused my taste buds to recoil at the very thought of it, but to deviate from the norm is considered a rejection of Jewish tradition.

The children are already on holiday, having barely even managed to get their schedules and copy "Welcome to First Grade" from the board, and we don't know when our birthdays fall according to the Hebrew calendar, but still we procure the traditional holiday fruits – pomegranates that are still unripe and tart, yellow dates that leave a course aftertaste on the tongue, apples dipped in honey.

Every year I say a few words at the opening ceremony for the *Shorashim* volunteer holiday drive, where members wrap care packages and deliver them to senior citizens, the needy and "multi-problem" families, as the social workers refer to them.

Addicts, prisoners, Holocaust survivors. A holiday care package containing frozen chicken and dairy products, honey, cookies and staple foods, so the holiday need not be cheerless or impoverished. I already know I won't be there next year to organize things and toast the staff of social workers and volunteers, because my position as civil servant has come to an end in these final days of summer. I had been: Chairperson of the City Council; Director of the Committee for Human Rights, Children's Rights and National Programs for Children at Risk; Active Director in the Israel Museum and at *Ir Olam* and the Association for Tourism; Member of the Finance Committee; Chairperson of the Society for the Disabled and The Disability Access Committee. I tried to protect what remains of the rights and dignity of African asylum seekers as Director of "The Refugee Forum," a role desired by none, and as "The mother of the Gay and Lesbian Community," I shared the community's joys, struggles, losses and the humiliation that transgenders still face as an ostracized group within the community.

I am ending my role unwillingly, an unsatisfying, unexpected explanation has been delivered in a laconic conversation, laced with compliments; and in the upcoming elections my name will be erased from the ballot.

You take the blow. You're hurt. The eyes water but no tears come. You are free from shame. You would be ashamed had you done something insufficiently, had an intention of yours not succeeded or a project failed. You take offence because the explanation for your rejection is unconvincing. You revisit the tough times when you worked vigorously for people who were appreciative, admiring and grateful, who grew alongside your efforts and brought home a formidable catch of fish with the skills you taught them, even if they didn't elect you. You have stopped anticipating rewards and you didn't expect to be adored, to be showered with gifts or recognition. Throwing you out because of what you are not, means that your expiration date has passed, that what remains of you no longer justifies a place on the candidate list.

You cannot fill the empty spot on the list, reserved for: a Sephardi, disenfranchised, someone young perhaps, who has firsthand experience of the plight of the poor neighborhoods, "the south" in Tel Aviv slang. You are nothing of those and do not "represent", and you are offended that your talents are not considered, your proven record of accomplishments, your independence and determination in tackling the issues and fighting for the causes that you believe in, which are probably a rare commodity too.

You are "the baby thrown out with the bathwater" in order to make room for new waters where other babies will grow, ones that represent, that are a better fit. You are bitter because you sense that their compliments are bland and banal, and their summing up sounds like a eulogy for someone unwilling to die. You didn't expect the sword to be thrusted on the branch still bearing fruit, a multi-seasonal bloomer, devoted entirely to serving the public in good faith, with commitment, without keeping tabs.

Bitter and restrained, the closing of a chapter in a book whose end has yet to be written opens, and you grieve the issues that took up much of your desk, issues that were cast aside by virtually everyone else. You are well-schooled in the ways of politics, knowledgeable in fickleness, and you know that everyone is replaceable, but you also know that you could have been accommodated. You think about the people you have served, responding to their needs and providing tangible results without a trace of arrogance, with loyalty and consideration and sometimes a clenching of the fists and a grinding of the teeth, accepting insults and physical abuse, lending every form of support possible to the asylum seekers, the Africans who are now "infiltrators" according to the law, seeking refuge in a country of former refugees who monopolize victimhood and have forgotten their own origins.

You label the expiration date on your slack arms and the wrinkled skin on your forearms, like grooves in a barren land. No one will be orphaned due to your dismissal, but you'll be cut off from the source of your contribution, and you are indeed, too old for a fresh start. You won't settle for charity on the outskirts of activity.

You accept the blow with no desire for revenge, only disappointment, for you know that there is a spark that hasn't been extinguished, and that it is lighting a new path.

I don't have much time left. There's certainly not enough for new beginnings. The next step from here, had it not been prevented, was not rewarding past work or accomplishments or exceptional marks. The next step was about keeping my promises, drawing on the knowledge and experience that I continue to amass and deepening my sense of compassion and empathy, which I didn't always possess. There were always and above all commitments to human-rights and peace. No force can drive me away from trying to reach a two-state solution to our conflict with the Palestinians and equality inside Israeli society, preferably by separation of the state from religion.

The surprise led to a state of insecurity, it was not the first time, but it will probably be my last in the public eye. Perhaps it is because of the High Holidays. Perhaps it is simply a coincidence that has to do with age, being incapacitated, my lungs and the cancer that dwelled within me and even though it has since taken leave, I still sense it lurking at the doorway.

I am not the woman I was a decade ago, or twenty and thirty years earlier, when I was elected a *Knesset* Member, or forty-five years ago when I married. I am another woman. But we share the same DNA, our brains weigh the same and we are both judgmental and demanding of ourselves and our surroundings, though to different degrees. I am several different women, different arrangements of the same piece of music, a different array of colors, different strengths and weaknesses, and not always in the evolutionary way of nature.

I haven't mutated every decade, but rather went through a repeated cycle of: encompassing it all, absorbing, emptying and releasing, while the vessel underwent changes such as menopause, depletion, exhaustion, seasonal blooming and autumnal fall. I know what I will not have the time to do.

I do not want to arrive anymore. I am prepared to remain on the other side. "A man and his Nevo / on a wide plain."[16]

I want things that are in my immediate vicinity – another birthday celebration for a grandchild, my granddaughters' transition to adolescence; I don't want to cross the finish line, just to get close. To move towards it on the course of my goals and my

---

16 Ra'hel "From Mount Nevo".

struggles: for peace, to banish ignorance and racism, oppose violence, human victories that are within our reach. I don't want to scoop it up in handfuls, I'd be content merely to touch it.

My mother and her mother found personal happiness within their families; they each had children, grandchildren and great-grandchildren, and Grandma Rachel even had great-great grandchildren too. Each lived for about a hundred years – witnessing the great wars, the Holocaust, the revival of the Jewish people, governments that rose and fell, the new inventions and discoveries that would shape the future, the separating walls that were erected and later torn down, the uplifting art that was being produced, the distances shortening, diseases being eradicated.

They did not live to see the great light, the experience of peace, gaps being bridged, and hatred for the other dissipating. Perhaps in such advanced years, the expectations for healing the world or tikkun olam are lowered, perhaps faint glimmers of satisfaction and the dignity of independence is enough, and the various disappointments are diluted in a pool of physical and mental fatigue. mother does not expect to see peace and witness the end of the conflict in her lifetime. Bitterness stains the joy of her final years.

"I can't bear it any longer," she sadly describes her attitude towards the occupation and the lack of an honest attempt to give peace a chance. For nearly a century, dreams have been shattered in the intolerable reality of arrogance and an indifference that disables their fortitude.

I am not there yet, not giving up behind closed doors. I want to be heard, to respond, to make demands and maybe even make a difference until I am certain that the goal will be attained. I want to leave behind a legacy of certainty, not a vision.

Sometime between *Rosh Hashanah* and *Yom Kippur*, the plants in the western window box shriveled up and died. The flowers crumpled and their color darkened, even the resilient gauras fell to the ground. "The magic mountain" spicy basil folded its leaves inwards, as if it had aged all of a sudden, losing its charm and intoxicating scent. Almost overnight, the fleshy leaves of summer that had once spread out and grown long, creeping and grasping at other branches, had dried up and now looked like discarded candy wrappers. The red kalanchoe barely survived, its flowers wilted and the leaves browned at the edges.

There is no explanation for the sudden wilting of all the plants. No scale insects were spotted, there were no moth holes in the leaves, or mildew, nor did they suffer from a lack of water or over watering too much salt in the air or pests in the soil, it was as if both of the bedroom window boxes simply decided to commit suicide.

Once again, Karel Capek offered comfort: "A gardener would like to think that his flowers grow so nicely due to an affection for him. There's something to it, in gardening you need to have luck or some kind of divine grace….amateurs such as ourselves fool around with germinating seeds, we wet them, blow on them, feed them like babies and finally, it somehow dries up and dies…I believe there is some kind of witchcraft to that,"[17]

---

17 Karel Capek, *The Gardener's Year.*

Transitions

The sad sight of the shriveled up remains of the plants added to my foul mood and sent a message to my atrophic lungs. I closed the blinds, shutting out the exterior world visible between the slats, and hooked myself up to the oxygen generator.

I gave up on the west and concentrated my attention on the window boxes facing east, where the acarina had raided, miniscule marrow-sucking spiders spun webs that clung to my dear pentas flowers, whose nectar provides the honey-suckers with their daily sustenance in the sticky webs I take apart and prune. I sprinkled a poisonous solution, watering them close to the roots and a day later, the acarina were defeated and the flowers recovered.

I walk around the house with an oxygen concentrator, transposed from my place as an initiator, a generator of action, to an object of it. I feel my hungry lungs, unable to take it all in, much less fully deflate. I try different positions, inhalers, bronchodilators until finally giving up. I have no doubt that my dark mood is directly tied to the blocked lobes of my lungs, compressing me inside my own skin.

Every morning I rise in anticipation of a new, healthier day that will unfold, but after taking the first few brisk steps, I need to stop and hang on to a piece of furniture, panting until I can sit down again.

At home I can maintain some semblance of independence, but it inevitably crumbles as soon as I venture out of the house. The smallest effort is enough to send the oxygen tubes back into my nostrils and deliver me into the loathsome, overindulging wheelchair.

I reexamine the effects of depression on cells and proteins, the body's dependency on the spirit and vice versa. Depression bolsters bone-destroying cells and increases osteoporosis. A bad mood doesn't inspire any form of physical exercise, weighs heavy on the body and its metabolism, which in turn strengthens a sense of apathy and the avoidance of activity and so forth. I search and the search brings about knowledge which leads to another cycle of frustration and depression and I no longer know whether it is the result of the illness or the cause of it.

I give up the obsession to read, take notes and summarize. I must separate the things I can still learn from those I cannot and which will remain unanswered. Not in the time I have left to live. I also acknowledge my desire to know, to understand the meaningless of the individual life, its cessation, death and not fear the impending future. Perhaps there is also the need to put off the sense of the end, which grows stronger with pain, infirmity, memory lapses and the deaths of people my age.

And perhaps the process is reversible. If I can manage to regain a sense of hope, passion, the anticipation of another day, maybe I will defeat the osteoclastic cells and the onset of depression, invigorate my bodily organs and infuse the intricate spirals of my brain with a healing, rehabilitating elixir to venture outside without the oxygen. The attempt fails soon after I cross the square and reach the fountain, and I must find a seat on the wood benches that flank it.

Chapter 8

Yom Kippur. War and Atonement. My father reexamined.

The period before the High Holidays is not the best time for changing moods or making decisions, and I am no longer the woman I was forty years ago.

I try to stifle the thought of the oncoming *Yom Kippur,* to avoid it, to run away – the way I managed to do last year when I sailed to the coast of Tunisia, Morocco and the Canary Islands. I am here now, and I cannot hide from my memories and mostly those of others.

The collective memory of the Yom Kippur War and the condemnation of my father increases each year and the intense, growing hatred is directed at me as well, as if I were a piece of tissue on the rim of the malignant tumor.

Every year I return to what became known as the "traumatic war." Forty years have passed, and the round, even number does not magnify nor does it diminish the residue left behind. Those who were killed in that war have not loved, failed, succeeded or had children.

Everyone who was injured has not forgotten, and those who carried on with their lives have bandaged their wounds and started counting their years anew.

What was consensual, or at least so I felt, was the hatred towards my father, hatred that scorched everyone in his vicinity, and the embers were reignited every few years and particularly each decade. Every book that was published, every reliable memory that was filmed or recorded; all were thrown into the burning fire. In time, the graves of the leaders joined the rows of the graves of the soldiers, and beside them stood the children and the orphans, preparing to defend and attack, to write and rewrite the roles of their fathers in that war, all innocent next to the huge pillar of guilt and shame that was my one-eyed father.

I find it hard to think back on a meaningful *Yom Kippur* before that war which crushed all of us. The blind and those who could see. I remember *Yom Kippur* in the Nahalal of my childhood and youth, and as is the case in many secular families, it wasn't a particularly notable event. We didn't feel the forced silence, the stillness of the media and the heaviness in the air, counting the hours until sunset. We drove to Nazareth to have a good meal, the roads were open to cars, and there was nothing inviting about the small synagogue in Nahalal. There would be a minyan of elderly men and perhaps one family, commemorating the day.

When the children were young, we would walk up the road from Ein Hod to the synagogue at Nir - Etzion to listen to the prayer and the shofar. Not in order to strengthen their faith, but to compensate for the lack of it.

Dov would take our boy's hand in his hand and our little girl on his shoulders; he did not speak or reminisce or draw any connections; he saw it as an educational task. An effort to dispel the confusion they could face when trying to reconcile the utter lack of faith in God with life in this holy land, beside Elijah the prophet and the Kishon Stream.

Dov did not fast and led an extremely different life than that of his childhood in rural Czechoslovakia, attending the Hebrew Zionist school at Munkacs. The holy books, the scholarly teachings of the weekly Torah portions and the depth of the Kabbalah were all covered by a thick, opaque dome of smoke that had engulfed them, burying his father, his mother and younger brother, burying God and laughter.

On the eve of that *Yom Kippur,* too, we returned home to Ein Hod, ate dinner and put the children to bed. The silence was pleasant because it was a matter of course, and not forced upon anyone. We halved pomegranates that grew in our backyard and cuddled underneath the blanket in the chill of the night air.

The silence was pierced at six a.m. with the ring of the telephone. I answered – I was always a light sleeper– and my father was on the other end of the line. "I suggest you return to Tel Aviv," he said. "Dov should get back to Tel Aviv and to his regiment, you can stay in Ein Hod with the children, but I think you will want to be here when the war breaks out."

Within minutes, we woke the children up and were all in the car. We drove on the small road that merged with the coastal road, the heavy Lark Studebaker was the lone car on the road, and arrived at our apartment in Ramat Aviv in under an hour.

Dov put on his uniform and drove off. I remember hesitating to inquire about what many did not yet know and what he meant exactly. Then came the sounds on the street and over the radio and I didn't feel as lonely.

The following day I phoned my reserves regiment, The IDF Spokesperson Unit. I was assigned the position of volunteer coordinator at the Tel Hashomer Hospital, I found a babysitter to stay with the children in the afternoons and began my service in the military reserves. I would've liked to have written "and the rest is history," but that isn't true. No one left that war the same way they came into it. Even the ones that weren't orphaned, widowed or seared by inconsolable grief, and did not accuse and weren't accused – came out hurt. That war caused the connectors of our double helix to digress. It was a mutation that would penetrate deeply, sustaining itself in each and every cell.

During the war, I saw my father several times only at night. I was busy, I had immersed myself in my role at Tel Hashomer Hospital, where I would coordinate volunteers to help nurse, entertain and keep the wounded company.

"Don't leave anyone alone" was the order as well as the heart's desire. Don't leave the caregivers and the volunteers alone either, rescue the rescuers too.

The harsh sight of burn victims, amputees, the blind with their eyes bandaged who will never see the light of day after being hit by the massive glare, all the sights were wrapped up in bundles and shadows when night fell, but the silence was interrupted by cries of pain, the murmurings of the delusional and the screams of the terrified.

I barely saw Dov. We took turns caring for the children, trying not to contaminate their innocence with the concern, fear and uncertainty that enveloped us. We mourned our friends, retreating to our separate corners, and we couldn't touch each other or find comfort in love. We were ashamed that we had love.

My father was tense and often angry and I only realized what he was going through some time later. Unlike his detractors, I didn't see him as defeated but determined, not broken but mobilized, down to his very core, intent on finding solutions.

My father spoke on television and over the radio, and even when he said the exact things as the others, it was obvious that his words had double and triple the weight, the power to raise to great heights or drag down to deep waters. He was not defeated, and as the story of Sisyphus, his is not one of defeat. It is a heroic tale, the power to fight, to keep rolling the boulder up the hill as long as strength does not fail you, not be crushed underneath its weight and learn the details of the track uphill. He did not pretend and he did not think that the truth could not be withstood.

The uncertainty of events that transpired, what some have been told and what others have seen, the different versions, the distortion and disinformation some of which hinted to the most unimaginable and dangerous conclusions haunted us throughout the years and prevented the wounds from forming a scab and healing.

You stayed at the hospital even after the war ended, remaining with the injured, the burn victims, the head trauma wounded, whose pain that could not be alleviated. The artists who came to entertain the wounded and ease some of the stress and pain would exit the hospital rooms in tears. And every night you would come home to a new, different experience. From the daughter of an almost embarrassingly admired hero, a "ladies man" and a role model for young fighters, you became the daughter of a "traitor," "murderer," an "architect of the military graveyards," as he was called on the posters and signs that were put up next to the house in Zahala and in public places.

In the first few years after the war, the wounds were fresh and people were busy rehabilitating their bodies and spirits. Slowly the voices died down.

They resurfaced with the publication of the Agranat Inquiry Commission report and the elections that were held in '77 when father joined Begin's right-wing government.[18]

The things that weren't written down by your father and were left unsaid by

---

18 The Agranat Inquiry Commission cleared the political leadership, including Golda Meir and Moshe Dayan, of responsibility for the failings of the Yom Kippur War.

other military men and investigators you knew and trusted, remained unclear to you, a mystery. Speculations, assumptions and conjecture, perjurious statements and outright disinformation, figments of the imagination and some grain of truth. You lacked the tools to clarify them or answer the questions.

You feel the inadequacy but cannot define it. It is something you do not know and perhaps do not want to know. You believed everything your father told you, but you didn't inquire further or insist on knowing the things he did not wish to share.

You read everything written, narrated and recounted about that war, adding to the information that you knew and sensed.

You were comforted by the investigative reports that provided proof of his clearcut foreign policy and stance on the eve of the war, and you never imagined that the accusations would continue, obsessively, ad infinitum. The purpose of the accusations was not reform, or to draw conclusions and change the procedure regarding the readiness of response and responsibility. They were aimed solely at perpetuating the wild dance with the scapegoat.

And they continued even as some of the accusations turned out to be false or fabricated, even when he lead the struggle for peace, even when several of his foreign policy assumptions, plans and assessments turned out to be accurate, even when he was exhausted, withering away and gravely ill, even when he died. Decade after decade, generation after generation.

And from the outset the accusations are directed at you too. Cheap, hurtful aggressiveness ignoring who you are, and took no notice of the person that he either was or wasn't. You were damaged, helpless, lifting your head every so often to open your mouth responding and defending.

Him? Yourself?

Even in the arid land we are not blessed with oblivion, and so, in these days between *Rosh Hashanah* and *Yom Kippur,* as the anniversary of the war approaches, not only the plants in the western window boxes wither away. You too disappear and remain voiceless and beg your soul to sever the umbilical cord that strangers have tied between you and him.

You loved him all your life and most of your life you feared him. He loved you and didn't particularly love life, "it's not how long you live but how well you live," he said to you as he leant against the fence of the abandoned cowshed in Nahalal. At a certain point your fear gave way to a soft compassion, not because he induced sympathy, but because it was you who had changed, you were able to contain more, you were less vulnerable, and perhaps the liberation from his authority opened you up to him and you were able to share secrets and knowing smiles.

Eight years and two weeks have passed between the Hebrew month of Tishri of that war and the Tishri of my father's death. Two years separate between the signing of the peace accords with Egypt and his death. Two months stand between his death and our son Dan's *Bar-Mitzvah.* Forty years have passed between that war and this autumn.

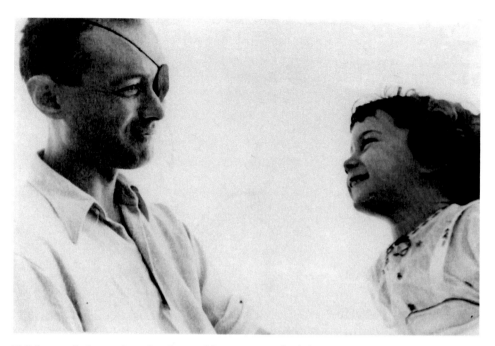

With my father after the loss of his eye. Nahalal, 1942

Ruth, Assi, Moshe, Udi and Yael, 1954

With my brothers Assi and Udi, 1962

With my father, Minister of Defense, on his visit to Sinai during The Six Day War 1967 (photo: Government Press Office).

At the launch of "Death of Two Sons", Paris, 1967

Wedding, July 1967

Honeymoon in Rome, Fall 1967 (Photo: Enzio Lucceri)

With my children,
Dan and Racheli, at
the house in Zahala
1976 (Photo: Yael
Rozen)

With. mother Ruth, my
grandmother Rachel
Shwarz, and my daughter
Racheli 1985.
(Photo: Mariana Cook)

At the Knesset podium speaking on "International Women's Day,
March 2000. (Photo: Government Press Office)

With Yasser Arafat, Gaza (1995)

With Hillary Clinton in Jerusalem, I am an M.P, she is accompanying her husband Pres. Bill Clinton

At one of the demonstrations protesting "A Futile War" - The Second Lebanon War, Tel Aviv (2006)

At 75, with mother at 97, 2014 (Photo: Yaira Yasmin)

With father, a year before his death at 66, 1981 (Photo: Yael Rozen)

Seder night (2014); last picture before Assi's death.

With my Grandchildren, Yasmin, Alma, Adam and Boaz at my home. Summer 2014. (Photo: Emelyn Lising)

Chapter 9

Knesset Member 1992-2003.
Am I a Patriot? A Traitor?

Eleven years after the death of my father I was elected as a Knesset Member. On account of his legacy or despite it.

Yizhak Rabin was Prime Minister at the time and I was a *Knesset* Member of the Labor Party. Some called me a "princess" grouping me with the short list of sons and daughters of former *Knesset* Members, but in fact, I was "third generation", as my grandfather Shmuel had been member of the first Israeli *Knesset* to be replaced by my father, and now in 1992 I was sworn in.

Until elected, I remained out of the public eye, despite taking part in demonstrations, protest rallies and political and social debates. During my first years in the Knesset, the connection between me and my father was not made. I was not held accountable for his failures, nor benefited from his gains. When we were hated, it was each of us in his or her own right. My share of negative sentiments was generally related gender-related; the expletives that were flung at me in various languages could all be reduced to the word "whore," to which the prefix "Arafat's" or "Rabin's" would then be added. Beneath the vulgar language and crude jokes, beneath the sharp tongues in the plenary and the full-hearted applause at the rallies and lectures, something evil was lurking.

It would later go on to rupture the delicate fabric of our being. Undoing the thin line between legal and religious decrees, between the humanistic equalizing of nations and peoples, the arrogance of a chosen people. Between the rapidly spreading sense of contempt that overpowered the sensible confidence in the hope to establish stable neighborly relations. Between "right" and "left" to use the terms of the 90s. Between those who violently coerce others and those that hope to accommodate them.

The rift was buried in the embers beneath the hot coals, waiting to be ignited. The evil and destruction swarming underground were disguised as fervent faith, rising above the Earth like a cloud of toxic steam.

Yael Dayan

The change that was about to occur did not wait in silence, nor was it announced with a blow of the horn, but emitted a wild disturbing growl, like an animal clawing its way in, upturning all of the foundations. The ground on which once the foot stepped surely had been dug up and blind moles scurried in the tunnels where all sorts of reptiles slithered, spawning and raising their ugly little heads with low, threatening sounds that were swallowed up inside the dirt, or the sand, or the piece of land that I it when thought came between good and evil. We were late in recognizing it, only identifying our sky had darkened, when the Prime Minister was murdered.

There were two occasions in which Itzhak Rabin grew very angry with me. He led the Labor Party, he was my Prime Minister and I was a new, although not young, *Knesset* Member in parliament.

The first time he became furious with me, I had unintentionally made a mistake. It was my first *Yom Kippur* as *Knesset* Member and I behaved, as was my habit every year, and found a good spot on the beach to read and tan in the final days of summer. I had visited Dahlia, who considered the sun an enemy, and left her apartment for the nearby beach, where I lay out on the sand with a book. I didn't see the camera lens, didn't speak to anyone, and obviously had no intention of being contentious, impertinent, or hurtful. I later returned to Dahlia's and when the fast ended, I went home.

The following day, the front page of one of the leading newspapers printed a photograph of me in a colorful bikini. Before I even laid eyes on the photo, I heard the Prime Minister's booming voice: "What do you think you're doing...This is the last thing I need right now...Your foolishness will lead to a crisis in the coalition...make a public apology immediately."

I hurried to do some damage control, a television appearance, an apology, I never meant to offend anyone, etc. etc. until things seemed to have calmed down.

Except they didn't. Throughout the years and to this very day, the event has been described, both in Israel and abroad, as a deliberate act of provocation on my part, an insult to Judaism and faith, a violation of sacredness and I was called a disgrace to my parents, my people and to those who laid down their lives so as not to desecrate the holy day. On the other side, there were voices of ridicule too. I received messages and phone calls from women suggesting that I start a movement and bring thousands of women to the beach with me on the next *Yom Kippur* so we could fight for freedom, including the freedom to wear a bikini on a holy day and for the female body to be displayed without cowing to religious oppression.

I didn't find it funny. I didn't see it as a symbol for a struggle and I never would've dreamed of going to the beach in order to stand out, provoke, or cause offence. Rabin was well aware of that; he believed me when I told him it was not deliberately done and he was more annoyed than angry. He was adamant that it was a stupid thing to do, unbecoming of my new stature as an "elected public figure".

Before long the Prime Minister had another reason to become very angry with me, however that was far from an innocent mistake. The law prohibiting meeting with Palestinians had been overturned, as promised, when the twelfth *Knesset* convened. I

72

received an invitation to meet Yassir Arafat in Tunisia and felt no need or desire to ask permission to do so nor did I consult with anyone about the matter; I saw the meeting as an opportunity to foster what I believed in: a direct, trust-building dialogue with Palestinians and other Arabs.

Prior to becoming a *Knesset* Member, I had participated in numerous such meetings in Europe and the Unites States, which were initiated by the governments of Holland, Belgium, Greece and Spain, universities such as Harvard, Columbia, Berkeley and Granada, and by various Jewish communities, including the reform movement, that felt that something was badly amiss in the Zionism they cared so deeply about.

Heated arguments led to an understanding of the dividing issues and of the common ground we shared, the dangers, the opportunities and the foundation of an agreement as to what lies within the realm of possibility and what will remain an unrealized dream. During those meetings there were no attempts to settle accounts, to assign guilt, determine who was the instigator or what side that paid the higher price. Processes were mapped out, potential areas of dispute were marked, there was an understanding of the lack of symmetry between Israel and the Palestinian authority and there was plenty of hope.

I was pleased to receive Arafat's invitation. The mediator was French TV and we had agreed in advance to give them exclusive rights to the story.

I flew to Tunisia from Paris and was greeted at the airport by Gibril Rajoub, who spoke fluent Hebrew due to the time he had spent incarcerated in Israeli prisons. He was courteous and respectful. Beside him stood a representative from the Tunisian Foreign Ministry, who stamped my passport with the required visa. It was my first meeting with Rajoub. I quickly realized that he was well-informed about me, my biography and the opinions I held. We drove to a suburb where the homes of Arafat and other PLO officials were located.

Arafat was away in the Gulf region and expected back in two days, and up until his return I stayed in the family home of Yasser Abed Rabbo and his wife, the writer Liana Badr.

I toured Tunisia and the vicinity of the city escorted by various companions, mostly high-ranking PLO officials, refugees from the wars of '48 or '67. We were all curious about each other, about the subtle nuances of various opinions we held and were not dogmatically fixated on history, allowing both our narratives be considered. Conversations with high-ranking officials drew us nearer to a kind of friendship that is still, to the present's unsettling times, able to withstand the upheavals of the events.

I find it hard to explain the sense of ease I have in Northern Africa. The "Levant" of Lawrence Durrell's The Alexandria Quartet, the poetry of Cavafy, the struggle for the liberation of Algeria, The Plague. The French language in all of its various dialects in the French Colonies, the diverse nature of the Mediterranean beaches from north to south and back to Seville, Barcelona and Marseille, abundant with flavor and music. I feel this way not because of the exotic charm of Marrakesh or the colonialist architecture that can be found in the neighborhoods of Alexandria and the edifices of Tunisia.

Not on account of the minarets and the turquoise tiles, but because of the unique blend. The melting pot failed in Israel; it has transformed into a struggle between the "weak" and the "over privileged," a North African European dish that was burnt on the outset.Perhaps it will still be able to rise and prevail but it will take another generation or two after the what is currently a wasteland of disrespect and an unwillingness to assimilate or be assimilated and burst forth with a courageous, unique concoction whose whole is greater than the sum of its parts.

I felt at home at the marketplace in Fez. Wearing a *galabiya* or toting a Chanel purse while enjoying a steaming bowl of couscous not far from the synagogue at Djerba, with Afif Safieh who declared, "Before we met I loved to hate you, and now I hate to love you," and with Faisal Husseini, whose father and mine had fearlessly fought one another and   we lectured together at reform synagogues in the US.

Over tea in Sidi Bousaid, Tunisia, we wove our hopes and aspirations before a breathtaking view of La Goulette and the Carthaginian ruins.

When Arafat returned from the Gulf we met for a private lunch in the garden at his residence. The preliminary meeting was designed for us to get better acquainted and there was a mutual sense of curiosity as we evaluated one another.

Arafat confirmed that my father had indeed extended an invitation via Fadwa Touqan, the poetess from Nablus. He explained that he had declined because he feared that Dayan was setting a trap for him. You were completely wrong about my father's intentions, I told him, and we compared the quality of fresh dates in Tunisia and Deir al-Balah near Gaza and at the same time, the Right of Return and the partition of Jerusalem. Arafat could not conceal his suspiciousness, which to my opinion, clouded his judgment.

Even when I agreed with him regarding Israeli withdrawal to the '67 borders and the evacuation of settlements, he continued to discuss the right of return, as proof of our unwillingness to bear responsibility for the Palestinian tragedy. He knew that I opposed the right of return, apart from a handful of cases that pertain to the reuniting of families and some other exceptions, but he repeatedly brought it up.

I had deliberately avoided mentioning certain topics; I tried to find common ground and my intentions were good. His eyes darted with wariness and I didn't consider it to be the right time to begin a reckoning; not about the terrorist acts that he instigated either.

After lunch, in the presence of other high-ranking officials, we spent several hours discussing politics at the organization's offices having a political discussion. We dived with the utmost honesty into delicate topics and I felt I was witnessing something new, devoid of hostility or pretense, something that had a chance to succeed.

What gave me hope was not the man himself, but the atmosphere that reigned, one that was shared by the men and women who were part of his m*ilieu. I approached with gravity, aware of my responsibility. Ever since I was elected a Knesset* Member, I was familiar with, and tired of, the stale argumentative discourse, speaking in slogans. At the meeting I witnessed an attempt to get at the truth, with all of the difficulties that it entailed– on both our parts–not to halt at the emotional and intellectual barriers but to try and disband them and make progress.

I placed a call to Israel from Arafat's residence, dialing direct. I spoke to my mother who was envious of me, and with several members of my party, colleagues at the *Knesset,* who expressed little enthusiasm when I told them of my whereabouts. I realized that the Prime Minister had "lost it" when he heard about the meeting. At that time, in Tunisia, I was unaware that somewhere far-off up north, the Oslo treatise was in stages of development and that it was matter of crucial importance that everything concerning it remain strictly confidential.

Rabin's reaction startled you. You hadn't expected praise or even curious interest, but the tirade came out of the blue. The Prime Minister said that you were threatening national security. Following him soon afterwards came the hostile media, jealous friends and the violent protest at the airport where you had to be escorted out by a police officer. In the midst of all the commotion, you also received flowers from Tamar Gozansky, from the Arab-Israeli party who came to greet you with your assistants.

You missed your father so at that moment! He had received a similar blow when he met with the poet Fadwa Touqan at the house in Zahala, requesting that she relay an invitation to Arafat. Your father knew very well what it meant to understand the other, the enemy, and overcome prejudiced sentiment. He was a bridge-building strategist, relying on the shared soil, the similar flora and fauna on both sides of the river. Your father, who was derogatorily called *Abu Gildah*, and a Bedouin bandit, understood the meaning of attachment to the land, *tsumud*, blood ties and the loyalty to family and tribe.

You were surprised but not offended by the reactions in your party and the public who called you a traitor defaming Israel. That was even before Oslo, which would mark you for years to come.

The slander was ridden with sexism. There was talk of a "slobbery kiss on the enemy's stubbly cheek" and much innuendo about sexual relations with the enemy, even including a reference to Eva Braun.

Rabin warmly embraced the other causes I took up. He supported my feminist agenda and my legislative efforts to secure equal right for gays and lesbians in the IDF and in the community, as well as my stance on human and civil rights. All those were genuinely supported by him sometimes at a price of disagreement with his religious partners and even members of our own party who asked-What is the hurry?

Sometimes, like my father a decade beforehand, he was amazed to discover the extent of discrimination and the widespread prejudices and obstacles that women encountered on the road to recognition, to affirmative action, to securing a deserved promotion or making sure their voices were heard. There were many strong, bright, opinionated women surrounding Yitzhak Rabin. He found it hard to recognize the impediments and obstacles that women faced when seeking equality, equal opportunity, the banning of discrimination and adequate representation.

I had rivals, adversaries and even violent opponents in my political life. However, the sexist attacks also served to fortify support and caused people to identify with me. My appearance, my face and my demeanor, which was never meek or hesitant, did away with cynicism and envy, and by and large– everything was out in the open and made public and I never stooped down to the low level of debate and the crass language of those who attacked me, not when seated at the table on a weekly TV debate, nor on the Knesset podium.

The insults and disgusting expressions, the threats in the mail or over the phone increased, alongside the general sentiment of incitement against the Arabs and the eruption of continuous violent messianic activity expressed in the building of settlements in the occupied territories, on stolen or confiscated land with a condescending attitude of chosen to rule and enslave a lesser people.

The hatred did not distinguish between a comprehensive social-democratic perspective that is multi-faceted and multi-colored, and its concerns and unique activities regarding peace and the conflict with the Palestinians. Women's rights, equal rights regardless of sexual orientation, the Yom Kippur War, preventing sexual harassment, representing women in all spheres, meeting Arafat in Tunisia, the secret Oslo negotiations– all of those made me arrogant in their eyes, too strong to take on, but weak enough to target.

I received envelopes with nine millimetre bullets in them, death threats and hate mail directed at me and my children, my front door was vandalized with abusive graffiti like "die scum" and statements such as "Yael Dayan is a homosexual" scrawled in paint and chalk. My friends in the gay community erased them. Everything was recorded and filed with *Knesset* security. Ezer Weizman, my uncle, (later elected President) sent me to get a firearm license and equipped me with a small Beretta for self-defense.

But it didn't stop. The remarks in the *Knesset* hallways, being cursed and spat upon on the street, the abusive taunts while I spoke on the podium . Usually, my father wasn't mentioned in this context. Sexual orientation, feminism, sexual harassment– those expressions didn't even exist in his mind set nor were they part of his agenda. He was neither for or against them.

They were nonexistent in his circles– in Nahalal or the commando units. Not with the Bedouins of the Mazareeb, the mayors in the West Bank and Gaza, not in the complicated relationship he had with the Arabs nor with King Hussein of Jordan and President Sadat of Egypt. I was targeted– and also praised–in my own right.

Dov came from other provinces. Although he belonged to the "generation of generals" he shared my struggle due to his natural disposition, which was tolerant, egalitarian and moral. More mature, educated, restrained and thoughtful than many of his colleagues.

In the political sphere he was skeptical, cynical and outspoken towards Rabin and Sharon, his commanders, as well as totally loyal. Loyal to his superiors and to those he commanded.

Dov was at my side when I was sworn in as a *Knesset* Member, although the first signs of disease could already be discerned. During the first two years of my term, he was fully supportive and took an active interest in my job, and as long as Yitzhak Rabin was Prime Minister, he felt that my path was paved with integrity, which he regarded as a supreme value.

I didn't share Dov's inherited ability to maneuver between Kafka and Hašek or his European sense of restraint. When his disease began to be present in our daily lives, I found it very hard to strike a balance between my home in Tel Aviv and the *Knesset* in Jerusalem.

Your children had left home and you and Dov had a damaged, unequal relationship, and you were torn between the two spheres of your disjointed life.

It was only during moments of crisis that you came to see the depth of the chasm and the how great the illusion was that you were "handling things". The loyalty of the Filipino caretaker, your health and vigor maintained the illusion that you were of benefit in the *Knesset* and as you skipped home almost every other day, you believed it follows a fixed routine.You were not in your element in either place and you were struggling to save a façade that was false, misleading yourself to believe you were in control.

You weren't alone in the *Knesset*. You had a support group; you were aided by government and party members and you were the only woman in the rebellious group of peace and human rights activists called "The Octet". You served on the Foreign Affairs and Defense Committee, the Constitution Committee, and founded the "Committee for the Advancement of Women" which included men and women from all factions, ardent feminists and male chauvinists. You headed this Committee for several years.

Perhaps it was really balanced and perhaps you avoided the issue but when the earth shattering political event occurred, with the assassination of Rabin, you were finally faced with the truth.

At home, in the world parallel to the realm of politics, you were alone.

When you informed Dov that Yitzhak Rabin had been murdered, in the city square, by a religious Jew– he did not react.

Every so often, when Dov gathered that I had returned home from the Knesset in Jerusalem, he would ask about Rabin and Sharon. He did not comprehend my truthful responses and in time I stopped trying to present him with reality for it only caused confusion and increased his suspicion.

There were a few moments during the final years of his life that Dov came back, and could join us, almost fully present, joyful and happy.

Racheli and her partner Yishay had set a date for their wedding. We decided to have the chuppa at home and Dov who was a proud, loving father, fully participated in the event. Yishay,in his wisdom and patience, cultivated a respectful relationship with Dov, and he was for me, as I'm sure he was to Racheli, a great source of support during the difficult years, and was much appreciated by all the branches of our complicated family.

Dov wept at Racheli's wedding, he wept when she graduated medical school, and again when he laid eyes on Alma, our first grandchild, and gently, with trembling fingers, caressed her tiny foot.

I am certain that during those moments, the powerful emotion of love superseded the lack of dopamine, and we basked in its beauty. I took the good moments as signs of an improvement in his condition, but they also indicated the missed opportunities along the tearful course of what could have been and was now gone, forever.

Chapter 10

1985 - 2003. Dov's prolonged death. Alone together.

It was a clear-cut diagnosis, the future being mapped out like a deterministic graph with no deviations. His age at the time he was diagnosed did not bode well, and as I learned more about Parkinson's disease so did my reservoir of hope diminish. Dov's brother, Zvi, himself an expert doctor, did his best to help, trying to find encouragement among the known and the researched, but the issue was one of rhythm not of cure. We tried to fool the disease, pretending that the damage was merely physical, and even as the hallucinations and forgetfulness arrived, the angry outbursts and the gradual erosion of the man he once was, I kept searching and did not give up. The initial signs of dementia isolated the two of us as if we shared a secret. We conversed in a language inaccessible to others, escaping like lovebirds to places that hid the sinkholes forming in his brain, in his memory and in his personality. I let him initiate the conversations, the detailed plans and the fragments of memory. "You remember" he would say, "on the bridge in Prague..." And with caressing eyes I would complete his descriptions of times before my birth, grateful to him for firmly placing me, imagined yet existing, in all the landmarks of his life.

Even when Dov became oblivious to what had happened to him, to his personality, body and senses, he did not wish to die, and the term "dementia" did not suit him at all. He never lost his wisdom, never babbled incoherently and never stopped loving me and our children. Who was I to darken his days and tell him that the living Dahlia, or the dead Zvi or the murdered Rabin, did not sit facing him or meet him on the boulevard or at la Coupole in Paris or at Piazza Navona in Rome? I was with him wherever he was.

And then he began responding only when the sun shined directly on him– like the days he saw our first granddaughter Alma, and his face lit up with that "Dov'ale's smile", the way he used to be, a different man. The wonderful doctor who cared for him did not try to sell us any illusions. He carefully listed the details of the disease, its course and the new developments and breakthroughs in treatment that Dov would have to miss out on due to his age and general health. I diligently read through the research and studies conducted even when they could be of no use to him, finding gratification in the ability of the mind to keep seeking relief, despite missing out on a cure.

The disaster that we endured for a decade, every day and every night, was not one we shared equally. We lived in the same house, sat down to the same table, we had two children and a granddaughter, a joint bank account, a large library whose books we read, we had letters that we saved carefully in a box, photo albums amassed for over twenty years, when we were both present, together and apart, in the joyful occasions as well as in times of sorrow, anger and separation. Two people, so different and loving, walking the same road holding hands or talking or in silence, when suddenly, halfway through, an abyss opens up or a hand is sent down from heaven, seizing Dov and transporting him to another land, and he is unaware of what is happening, of where he is taken and of the magnitude of the disaster befalling us, unaware that we have lost one another forever although we are living together as partners, and are parents to a son and a daughter, and grandparents to a granddaughter.

But we are no longer together. He is in his own rooms and his own world, the nature of which I cannot fathom, and in his own thoughts, of which I know nothing, whether they carry him anywhere at all, and where to; he is in his awful adaptation mode, which does not ask, or fight or tell of what will be. I am in my room, my world, my work and my loneliness, which is a form of relief too. I have no need to share the things I don't know and don't understand, including self-pity, which constitute comforts of sorts and offer me closure, the guilt that I have, which gives me strength to look for an inkling of meaning in the hopelessness that surrounds us. He is in his prolonged death and I in my standstill life.

Not that my life had come to a standstill. To wit, I do all the things that Dov doesn't do, as well as those that I always did on my own. What did come to a standstill was the partnership of all that we had together. This did not merely diminish or become deficient, but actually vanished from any talk of the future, of course, but also from that of the present, and I find myself talking about "my children," "my house," with these linguistic conjugations anticipating something foreboding and inevitable.

The lack of any hope of improvement showed in the caregivers' work, and Dov becomes more and more a body that is passive, delicate and fragile, in constant need of oiling and maintenance. When routine life became a matter of maintenance, I would, for most of the day, close the door connecting his rooms to mine, which had always been open, and through the gap I could see him moving to the bathroom and the dining table, shuffling by, walking with assistance, and in later months in a wheel chair for fear that he might fall. Through the opening, I could hear his painful moans and his wet cough, which would increase until he would choke when swallowing, food going down the windpipe rather than the esophagus. His face would turn blue and his breathing would stop, and Edgardo, his full-time Filipino caretaker, would expertly yank out whatever was stuck in his throat, or fold him over and cause him to cough it out, and I would stand by helplessly, patting Dov on the back, in true panic, knowing that someday such choking would mean the very end. Through the doorway, before I shut it, he saw me too, standing in the hallway, beside the desk, or in front of the computer, tending to my business. When he would leave the room he would turn towards me, indicating with his hand that he was aware of my presence.

When he was in the wheelchair, he would motion for it to be wheeled towards me. What went through his mind during the days I wasn't at my desk, and what did he think I was doing when he saw me there, or imagined seeing me there?

When the door was open, I would watch him being wheeled to the shower every morning. The naked body, covered in a robe in winter and a towel in summer, shrinking uncomfortably, protecting his private parts. He would to fight the caretaker in the shower. He would seize Edgardo's hands with his own, strong, beautiful hands, the most beautiful part of his body, digging his fingernails, which only I would be allowed to clip, into the tanned arms, yelling my name as he would sometimes call me then, Ya, Ya, and he in English HELP, not as a plea but with rage. "Get the gentile out of here," he demanded.

Even with the door closed I could hear him, and I'd come and speak to him as if he were really there, as if he could hear me well, recognizing and knowing, and who is to say that he didn't? When two more caretakers were added to the team, they became close to Edgardo, and would converse and chatter on their cell phones. Dov looks at them, and I feel that he can't identify them or tell them apart, his face a cross between bewilderment and fear. I would explain to him that R or K or E or G, each in their own shift, were kindhearted and were there to help, and he'd press my hand and refuse to let it go, and I knew that he had no idea who those people were nor what machine he was hooked up to via the tube in his stomach that he would yank out from time to time.

At times I tried to talk about the things that were able to rouse him momentarily with a smile I managed to force out – Dan, Racheli, our granddaughter, baby Alma… And just when it seems that he is with me he says, "Zvi is supposed to come over too," but Zvi, his brother will not come. He died of a serious illness in the spring, three years earlier.

The fear that gripped me in the face of dementia slowly dissipated. When we were alone in the room and he would confidently describe people he met and conversations he had, pleasant places and nice objects of art, I joined him whenever he wanted, in Sienna, in Prague, in an argument with the UN officer while visiting Taba in Egypt. He spoke softly, secretively, also about his secret activities, about London, about Marseilles, about his Dutch colleague and about the source in Lebanon. In all of these tales what he said was in encrypted code.

He retained an incredible sense of control, and had I desired to uncover even a little bit more, and I didn't, I had no doubt that his that he still retained the mechanism of secrecy. The gentleness and softness of his personality were still there when he spoke of Dalia's daily visits, the ones that had taken place and those that hadn't, of a gift from his brother that he received in the mail, or of the lunch he had had the day before at a fancy Indian restaurant in Paris.

The story of his brother's life and the love and affection towards him were at the very end of what we had together –when Zvi died our paths had already parted. I travelled to Zvi's family in Detroit to visit his grave, while Dov remained behind, in some other somewhere, awaiting his return. His younger brother was the only remnant from the close family, from the village and from Auschwitz, and in time I stopped trying to claim that Zvi had died, and Dov never revived any of his family members who perished, not even in his most delusional moments.

The luxuries of dementia did not pamper him.

I open the closed door almost every hour. Dropping in unexpectedly, testily, irritating his caretakers and distressing myself. When Dov is asleep I want to know why he isn't awake and when he's awake– why he isn't sleeping. I check the connections of his feeding tube, and when necessary, the oxygen tube too. If he needs to get a shot I administer it myself and wet his lips with a gauze-covered tongue depressor dipped in lemon, or coffee, or water, and he enthusiastically sucks at the forgotten flavor, which does not quench his thirst.

***

At night, between his dimness and your darkness, you enter his room and feel the temperature of his brow. He is sleeping and his eyes are closed, or half-closed, and you are void of thought, emotion or memories. Sometimes, at this hour of the night, he grasps your hand tightly in his, raises it to his lips, kisses it, and the tear in your eye is one of frustration mixed with rage, and not one of sentimentality or compassion. You plump up the pillows, straighten his covers and return to your room, defeated by mind- dulling exhaustion. Outside there is a deceptive kind of silence belonging to a city feigning sleep. A silence that is unsurprisingly pierced by the howls of a cat in heat or a barking dog, or the sirens of an ambulance as it makes its way, not to you, and by the measured steps of the late-nighters.

Sticky and nauseating hot air wafts through the slots of the blinds, row by row.

The roses in the window box are paltry and pathetic looking, and behind them a streetlight is doing its bare minimum, shining a dull yellow light. A dusty Ficus drops its fruit noisily on the hoods of the parked cars, and fruit bats traverse the sky like bad omens.

And then, the expected nightmare occurred. Dov fell at home, was found writhing in pain and was rushed to the hospital. While the doctors were discussing the possibility of surgery and I was quickly making arrangements to get a court's consent for such a decision, he lost consciousness, Racheli called a resuscitation team and they managed to get his pulse back but he was kept under induced coma and respiration to alleviate the pain from the fall.

When he was taken off of the respirator and opened his eyes it was enough for me to announce, "we're going home." I knew that a long stay in the hospital would deprive Dov of the tenuous grip he still had on what was familiar and connecting, and even the end of roads can take on a form of the scent of jasmine, a down comforter and a loving caress.

We returned to the previous routine, my nights tearful and sleepless.

The day's routine is now devoid even of the tastes it had before the fracture and the resuscitation, and what remains is the body and flow of substances through it. The future, as a component of the time axis common to me and my husband, does not exist. What remains is the present, his prolonged death.

In the morning they would hook his stomach up to the hollow tube, pumping thick, high-calorie matter rich in protein and dietary fibers, at a rate of 200 cc an hour. Everything the body requires to sustain it, said the doctor.

Late in evening they would disconnect the feeding tubes, and two people would lift him out of the armchair and into bed. He cannot stand on his feet, his legs are ghastly thin.

In bed, they change his diaper and prop him up with pillows so as to minimize the friction with the bedsores. The light is shut off, the guardrail on the hospital bed raised, Dov is now clean and loaded up with medication and food, but he cannot sleep. He lies on his side. Obedient and meek, positioned just as they have arranged him, his eyes are open and whether or not he hears me, he remains unresponsive. My hand is in his, and he presses it with a spark of recognition, and I think I see his lips moving when I say "good night." Or perhaps they don't.

When we are together we are not alone. Edgardo is in the kitchen or in his room He does not tamper with our privacy and I am grateful for his instinctive discretion.

I stroke Dov's forehead and retire to my room which smells different and has the pictures that I love on the walls, a beautiful carpet and an abundance of books. Dov never sleeps in my bedroom and if I could go back in time to "before" when it was still our bedroom, even though he'd probably have considered it too cluttered, it would've been to his liking. I go to bed late, after finishing up work and reading, unfocussed, and after a session of staring at various television programs. I wake up early after a dream- filled night and an uncomfortable, restless sleep, and turn to Dov's room to jump-start the routine of his new day.

The night's tired loneliness is replaced by the irritated loneliness of the morning. I wake the night caretaker and Edgardo with some effort. Five mornings a week in normal times, when I spend two nights in Jerusalem, and seven mornings when the Knesset is in recess.

My days and nights move on two circular tracks with different gravitational centers, and I am tossed from one to another according to varying degrees of urgency, over which I have no control. Along the track with Dov at its center I navigate purposelessly, like a spaceship loaded with memories and emptied of plans, sticking to the course even as gravity decreases and slackens, waiting, with no sense of longing, for a "small bang" to take me off course.

Yael Dayan

The other track that I move on is elliptical, moving alternatively towards and from the center that is not a source of heat or light but rather a point that creates a sense of responsibility and commitment. From the Knesset plenary hall to the committees, to legislation meetings, to bill proposals, to my very pleasant office, to the hotel room that is merely a hotel room, without personality or charm, functional – a key with a number. I check on things in the other track by phone- calls.. Years ago, it used to be conversations with Dov. On the nights that I would stay in Jerusalem he would be suspicious and impatient. Afterwards, when his condition worsened, he was either indifferent or aggressive. When I felt that the telephone conversations were confusing him, I would drive back to Tel Aviv for a brief reassuring conversation, and then return at night to Jerusalem and the hotel room.

Driving at night up from the Tel Aviv plain to the Jerusalem hills, from the humidity to the dryness of the air, sometimes into a fog, or heavy, visibility-obstructing rain, I had the time to move from the circle of sadness and grief to the other sphere of my life, where every day required foresight, careful planning and an attempt to tackle both the very large-scale and the very small-scale issues of our lives. My own life moved along as if I had a split or double personality, and neither side was immune from internal strife. When I tried to live in both worlds and at the same time separate the two, Dov remained outside the realm of my public life. My days were partitioned into "home days" and "on-the-job days," but unsuccessfully so.

However, all of Dov's days are identical and he no longer asks, as he used to, "is today Friday?" being unaware of the difference between a weekday and *Shabbat*, and can no longer tell the difference, until told so explicitly, between waking up in the morning and rising from his afternoon nap, after which he would be wheeled for a walk to the promenade on the beach or the nearby boulevard.

When his body is scrubbed and washed by unfamiliar hands he musters all of the strength remaining in his arms and tries to resist and push them away. I can feel his sense of shame and dependence. I do not know if he feels pain, but surely there is pain in forgetting who he was, in trying to understand where he is and in making sense of this ever-lasting moment. And it is my pain too. That I know who and what he used to be, the man I loved, and what has become of him now, object of my compassion, and how he grows apart from us with this daily routine, walking in unmeasured steps towards a chaotic existence parallel to our own, for Parkinson's is not a terminal disease but a disruptive one, and I slowly, sorrowfully, learn Dov's new language, the shrunken and detached handwriting, the pathways of a dopamine-deprived brain, and I accede to his delusions for the chance to feel close to him, to touch him.

For a week now you feel that the end is near, the end of his life and the end of his death. You hang on to every spark in his eyes, any glimmer of recognition as if that's where the good news will start, and some kind of path that you have hitherto been unaware of will suddenly open up and transform a shred of a smile into a hearty laugh.

You speak to him, the caretakers speak to him, everyone knows that he is fading away and his breath becomes laborious and he is closing in on himself, and the circle of life is closing in on him, and hope, in this final week, is getting fainter. You reassure yourself by pretense. "How is Dov?" ask the people who ask. "The same," you reply. Yet the end doesn't have the same face as the prolonged end. You feel a constant sense of dread, in your chest and your knees, and emptiness in your head. In this final week you take leave of Dov in a different kind of way. You do not think of the future without him. You don't think of what used to be, or of what the two of you used to be, nor of what almost was, or how things will be after his death, you are focused solely on the present days and moments. He is the way he is and you are the way you are, in the paralyzing fear of a fall that ends not with a crash–but with an awakening.

The doctor came by on Sunday and diagnosed low oxygen saturation levels in his blood. His pulse and blood pressure were normal, but nevertheless something was different. The candle wick of his life, which once shone light upon him and those around him, which was thick or narrow or quick or restrained according to his will, now crawled duly towards its end. He looked at me and he saw me and recognized my face but his expression did not change. Our two-year-old granddaughter, Alma, visited every day walking towards him with a sure step, murmuring "Grandpa Dov" and waving at him, and his face would light up at the sight of her; a sort of smile of gratitude.

The little one showed him her boots, decorated with leaves, and he extended his limp hand to touch them. "Grandpa is sick," she said, without fear, and looked at him as they placed him in bed and covered him up, and she said good night. She watched my hand caressing his thin hair and asked to be stroked too. It has been his sign, every day for the past week, the single indication of a moment of grace and contentment. A crooked, sometimes toothless smile and a gurgling tongue. A faint glimmer in his lost, dull eyes as he focused upon her, and a failed attempt at raising a weak hand to touch and caress her. Each day of this last week I feel that I am quietly, lovingly, growing closer to him, not in order to go somewhere with him, but to say goodbye. The smile that stretched across my face through the tears did not wish him Godspeed, nor was it a facial souvenir for him to take with him, but rather a farewell smile, so I can remember myself like that, without suffering, without pity, the smile safeguarding the secret of our love.

A cold week of rain and hail. The wheelchair broke down, and the heating collected the bad odor, mixed up with cigarette smoke and disinfectant. Time is no longer measured in days, but in hours and I enter Dov's room and watch him, like a voyeur or a spy. I touch him. Check for signs of life. He still loosely presses my palm and follows my movements with his pupils when I ask him to, but uncontrolled indifference takes over him, over his hands and eyes, and over his body, which sinks into the chair without trying to alter its position. The caretakers now exhibit a special fearsome concern for the end, and they have now bonded over a new kind of compassion and closeness.

On the fourth day of the week, his breathing was burdened by phlegm and saliva and we finally managed to pump it out and offer him some relief.

The wheezing stopped; he looked well and fell into a peaceful night's sleep that lasted until mid-morning. I also treated myself to a morning in bed, in effect, succumbing to my reluctance to get up and begin tackling the day's obligations.

Edgardo and the other caretaker washed Dov, gave him his daily dose of medication, hooked him up to the feeding tube, and towards noon they began dressing him to go out on that clear, warm day. Then all of sudden the world went dark.

"He's not breathing," Edgardo came into my room, pale, shouting shakily. I ran to his bed. Dov lay there limply, not responding to my voice or to physical contact. I pressed the emergency alert button and asked for immediate intensive care to be sent over.

"What exactly is the problem?" asked the woman on the other end of the intercom.

"He's not breathing."

"The emergency mobile unit is on its way. Can you perform CPR?"

Edgardo, the caretaker and I began pumping his chest, getting instructions from the woman on the other end. "Keep going. Do it hard, at a steady pace. Does he have a pulse?" she asks.

The caretaker continued to pump his heart, Edgardo and I search for a pulse on the sides of his neck, and I ask-scream into the intercom, "where is the emergency mobile unit?"

The woman explained that there were none available at the time, and that they transferred the request to MDA (Israel's Red Cross). Ten minutes passed. Fifteen. The oxygen generator is inserted into his nose, the cardiac massage continues, the blood pressure monitor is not working and Dov's pupils are unresponsive. "Are they still not there?" asks the woman on the intercom.

I stopped answering her.

I can't really find a pulse, or a sign of life, or a response, nor do I know what to do and what not to do, and I call our daughter Racheli asking her to come over. I instruct Edgardo to go downstairs and wait for the ambulance, and desperately pound the broad chest belonging to the man who already seems dead to me by the time the paramedics arrive. They do their job professionally, but arrive extremely late.

Dov is lowered to the ground and given an injection, and then another. He is hooked up to an ECG device, and oxygen is pumped into him. Low saturation returns, as do an indication of blood pressure and a heartbeat. Another injection, Racheli arrives and we move Alma and her nanny to another room and then send them home– calmly and quietly. The emergency team places Dov in a chair, and gathers all of the apparatus, the oxygen and whatever is left of me, after my emotions are drained and my mind continues to function with precision, sticking to minor details and avoiding the essence, everything is loaded into the ambulance and the sound of the siren prevents me from hearing them explain why they were so late.

In the hospital, I follow behind the gurney as the paramedics reports the treatment details, the medication and the vital signs belonging to this man, who lies there with nothing about him exuding life, and amidst the incessant discussion and the chatter, all of him indicates – end. At the entrance to the Emergency Room and the Intensive Care Unit an angry looking doctor pushes me out, as if it were none of my business.

Transitions

We wait outside, the family and the caretakers.

"We've been through this before, and he managed to regain consciousness and go home," I try to remind myself with a flash of hope.

"It's not the same," says Racheli.

"Not at all," explains the senior doctor who knew us from Dov's previous stays at the hospital. Dov has suffered cardiac arrest, and resuscitation came late so it's very likely that his brain has suffered serious damage. New territory for us – cardiac arrest, potential brain damage. Short words, brutal and blunt, words with no intermediate shades, no twists or turns.

There is nowhere to hide from those words. They do not have a shoulder to lean on or a lap to curl up in with sorrow, and their reality lies beyond comprehension and tears.

Motionless, open eyelids, a limp body and a respirator connecting the wide, beloved body to a screen with the fluctuating line, which was now, alone, the sole indication of Dov's existence.

From the respirator, to the tube, to his throat, and to another tube tightly bound with cord, does oxygen flow – and this is his life. Dov is a transit station with no life of his own. Another tube, the feeding tube, leads from his nose to his stomach and this tube is also his life, running through a carefully controlled drip. And where this tube ends–like the IV in his vein pumping medicine and fluids– is where his life's vital signs end. And what is displayed on the screen are not Dov's vital signs, like the urine drainage bag and the blood pressure and pulse monitors, but the result of the tubes that oxygenize and nourish and secrete for him. The body, the living being, has become another sophisticated point of transfer that turns oxygen into heart and lung activity, into a reservoir of fluid that the kidneys cannot filter properly, generating swollen edema, and what is secreted is a concentrated trickle of urine that will never manage to fill the bag at the end of the catheter.

His pupils remain frozen, expressionless, even as I wipe the secretions from his eyelids, the same way I gently separate his lips from his teeth, moistening them with vaseline, in a futile, unnecessary attempt at grooming and cleanliness. Toxins fill his body and the organs are failing, destroying everything that existed in the space between the tubes and the machines. Dov is an illusion provided to us by the generosity and compassion of modern medicine.

It was impossible to imagine that Dov would regain consciousness, and even the doctors, with their words and hand-wringing gestures didn't foresee any chance of that happening.

I did not entertain false hope, I was impatient and nervously counted the hours remaining until it was all over. The "at least he's not suffering," statement, uttered by knowing doctors and friends attempting to find comforting words, became meaningless. Like the little boy in *The Emperor's New Clothes*, our son Dan asked, "How do you know he's not suffering? Maybe there's something inside him that is entirely inaccessible to you, located in an internal core and it can sense things." He feared that there was some intention, and there was none, to disconnect the tubes and hasten the end.

Racheli considered it somewhat cruel to suppose that it is an act of grace to allow the body to slowly destroy itself, soaring to high temperatures, with its subsystems damaged and flooded by contaminating toxins.

Perhaps the pain of a damaged organ and the suffering of a collapsing body system exist in themselves, even if the nerves transmitting the pain and turning it into sensations comprehensible to us have stopped functioning.

Our professor friend understood both Dan and Racheli. He explained that patients are not removed from respirators; neither as an act of grace nor as a prerogative.

Suffering is not prolonged, but neither does one treat that which is irreversible, and the family has time to part from the body of their loved one, slowly, and with the understanding that he is not suffering, and that our own suffering is tempered and mitigated since we still have something of Dov's with us.

You listened to the explanations about Dov's body with serious interest, and a certain degree of belligerence towards his attending physician. When he searched for the words intended to comfort you, you allowed him to do so. He lowered his eyes and spoke of "forty-eight hours," treading with caution and pity on the path of bad news, and you leveled your gaze at him, asking for details, separating the parts of the brain into cerebral cortex and brainstem, demanding information about causes of blot clots, creatinine and urea, you asked for signs about what is not and signals for what would never be.

Chapter 11

Crossing the river Styx. A new count of time.

The forty-eight hours passed, and the doctors, feeling cheated, mumbled, "He's very strong," and added another forty-eight hours to the number allotted to his life. I visited the ward every few hours in order to hear the same tedious words about his condition: it's the same, irreversible, he's not suffering, be strong. Each in their own way tried to help me take another step on the road to the inevitable, yet the soles of my shoes were already totally worn out walking this road, and I had already reached that inevitable end, me and Dov's body, his frozen pupils and tumid hands.

During the first few hours I thought it was best to hasten the end, and if everything was indeed completely irreversible, than perhaps it is best to have mercy on the living-dead rather than allowing them to keep fluttering pointlessly at death's door.

But the longer the moments, hours and days stretched, the more I felt that it was a time of grace. Not the prolonging of unnecessary torture but a dignified farewell.

The Prime Minister, Ariel ("Arik") Sharon, Dov's close friend, asked to come and say goodbye. He was apologetically shy. "I want to touch him, even if he isn't conscious, it's for my own sake," he said. We stood at round his bed, Dan and Racheli, Mother and Edgardo, me and the sympathetic doctor who was caring for us. Arik told the children about the adventures of "Dubon," hesitantly wiping away a tear. Stroking Dov's warm forehead and holding his hand emotionally, smiling at him. The words were elegiac, but the body is still warm and Dov is with us. His arms are warm and blood courses through them. His pupils do not move, he cannot hear and we don't speak to him, but he isn't really in freezing wet ground, and there isn't the commotion of death surrounding him, no whispering or shoveling clods of earth or Aramaic words uttered, and he is not returned to dust, nor to nothingness, or to "the afterlife." We were with him and his body was with us in this world, the only world, which has given us the grace of the good years and the bad years and the final days of parting, which too have their dignified routine.

Yael Dayan

Alma comes over every noon, Edgardo takes care of the cooking and cleaning, he airs out the bed-linen and looks after the dog, and he knows that Dov will not come home again but we do not discuss it. He has his own way of saying goodbye, in the silence of prayer, perhaps he saying goodbye to me and the family as well. We speak about the terrorist attack in Haifa, about the Gulf War– that will or will not take place.

At night he leaves me on my own and returns in the morning with fresh-baked rolls, and in time to walk the dog.

And a few days later you become patient and do not wait anymore. You are beyond the end of that road. You are flooded with the realization which had always been there deep inside, that you two would never grow old together. That the twenty year age difference, which you had always shrugged off with a confident smile, will leave you after his death at a good old age, a lonely widow forever in the face of your children and grandchildren; unless you die before him, which is no longer to be expected. Along with the certainty of his imminent death, comes the inevitability of your existence as defined by absence, in the many or few years that you have left.

***

A sun-kissed Saturday, ten days into this new count of time. The morning nurse chants: "the same." The evening nurse, inspired by the darkness and the silence, says, "he' s calm, very calm." The lines on the monitor shine nervously, soar to great heights, climbing up to a steep hill and reaching towards the next summit. The pulse is steady, the blood pressure low, and the only apparent change is the meagre amount of urine and the swelling of the limbs. The legs are scrawny as usual, the swelling in his arms and hands has increased, but is not repulsive to touch, and his facial hair is growing.

If the medical evaluations are erroneous, perhaps everything could still change. I don't really think these thoughts or expect anything to happen, but I allow my mind to linger without grasping at any concrete hope. I am not suffering, and the time that remains is not bothersome to me now. A buried body is taken apart by the forces of nature that reside outside of it, whereas Dov is subjected to the toxic chemical forces inside his own body. His warm frame, artificially ventilated, and the pulse that I can see throbbing at the sides of his neck and can sense with my fingers on his wrists, are not a point of no return, not the final end.

In the bed across from him, a woman has died. "Passed away," says the nurse, as she ushers the sobbing relatives into the narrow space behind the curtain. "Passed into her own world," as the Hebrew aphorism goes.

Dov will not "pass into his world", and there is no "world" to receive him, and his world is our world and it will miss him, long for him, consisting of flashes of memories supported by pictures and letters, a kind of memory that has no lessons to teach and no present or future, and what is happening in these recent days is also a memory, for we are not sharing the experiences with their object. Dov is no longer with us, only his body graces us.

I have time and am alone in the empty apartment. Absentmindedly, I make minor mistakes. I jot down numbers in the wrong order, go to the kitchen only to forget what I needed, pour milk from a closed carton, look for things that I placed in their usual spot and don't find them, and then obsessively rearrange the contents of a drawer until it's in meticulous order, clean out my desk and move on to sort Alma's toys.

Loving friends call to offer support, marveling at my strength and courage, and I try to explain, again and again, that the strength is nurtured by the struggle, and runs out when it is no longer needed.

I do not visit the ward in order to be with Dov but out of respect for my children and my friends, for the efforts of the doctors and the patience of the nurses.

"Nevertheless, it will be a relief once it is over," blurts out a close friend.

No, it will not be a relief. Dov cannot tell the difference between what is easy and what is impossible to bear. I will never, ever, feel relieved by the irreversible. Dov did not suffer and did not wish to die, I created an illusory world to which I was becoming accustomed, and I all I wanted was his life, in any form that it took.

Even Dov's death has circles of life to it. The circle of the difficult years, the circle of the even more difficult years, the circle of his slow death, and now the final circle leading to the void. And perhaps there are a few more days in store for him? He has defeated the doctor's predictions and the "average" odds. A statistical anomaly, a victorious deviation from the educated hypotheses, the preeminence of man, the preeminence of Dov.

Even if they do not last long, I am indebted to these days for disrupting my faith in the fact that through two points only one straight line can pass.

Dov's body temperature, which skyrocketed past 40-41 degrees Celsius, has gone down again. "The fever indicates that there is irreversible damage to the brainstem system responsible for body heat regulation..." The swelling that had distorted his arms, –particularly the right one– to repulsive dimensions, transforming his lithe long fingers into shapeless, swollen hunks of meat, decreased. "The edema clearly points to acute renal insufficiency that cannot be endured for more than a few days..." The bleeding from the opening of the feeding tube, which soaked through the gauze and the hospital gown and caused the doctor to summon Racheli, me and the surgeon from intensive care, so we could all be present in the final moments, stopped. "The bleeding probably indicates a decrease in coagulation factors which could be massive and lethal..."

Every day that goes by, and every night, is another straight line passing between two points, and we gently draw back the eyelids to examine the frozen, inactive pupils and the screen that flickers with the cardiac cycle and the pulse counter displayed in bright yellow. No change.

It is March 2003. Dov is dying and the world proceeds in sharp, cyclical movements, without reason or any realization of hopes. The US is on the verge of war in Iraq, over here we face the dread of the occupation, close to home and barred from the heart, and it is a joyless Purim holiday. The Arab population of Hebron is under curfew, as if they do not have enough of a curfew on their bodies and spirits, and they are sentenced to watch the shameful senseless spectacle of a mask parade of unrestrained hubris.

In the final three days of Dov's life, American forces invaded Iraq, the first war that Dov will not clarify for me, and I am already detaching myself from his deathbed and get caught up in the events of the hour.

Rachel Corrie, an American peace activist from Washington state, "met her maker" on the outskirts of Rafah, killed by an armored IDF bulldozer as she was trying to prevent a home from being destroyed. Two-year-old Hanan Al-Bassar was shot and killed by IDF soldiers who assassinated a high-ranking Hamas official in a neighboring apartment in the Nuseirat refugee camp. Thirteen-year-old Muhammad Darwish and seventeen-year-old Muhammad Abu-Youssef were killed in Al-Attara in an operation that also killed three armed men. A fifteen-year-old boy was killed in Tulkarm.

Edgardo requested, and I obviously approved, the sealing of an inner room for him in the apartment, so that he could alleviate his fears with the aid of Dov's special advanced self-ventilating gas mask. The room was also equipped with a flashlight, a transistor radio and bottled water, a television and instructions in several languages, and courtesy of Dov, who was in another world, sealed both inside and out, it also had an oxygen generator and a good quantity of first aid supplies..

The newscast programs added a stopwatch on the bottom of the screen. The numbers counted down the distance, in seconds, to nothingness, as if it led to the finish line of a race that had a winner and a prize affixed to it. It is 29:30:05 to the end of the ultimatum, a new countdown that ran from Wednesday to Thursday until the final hour of 00:00:00, and another Presidential address, and Home Front Command giving out their instructions on a rainy Thursday. Two weeks from Dov's hospitalization, where the stopwatch of his life had not yet stopped, but continues to add hours to his existence.

And the doctors, in their wisdom or ignorance, have given up on assessing just how many.

Special sprinklers were installed at the entrance to the hospital, looking as if they were designed to water a field of roses, and guarded by soldiers in the military reserves. More soldiers were posted in each of hallways and entrances to the hospital, prepared to treat the wounded, ready to mobilize all of the wheeled gurneys. Each one had a cardboard box kit slung over his shoulder, because the order had already been given to carry the gas mask kit around at all times and even to open it in order to "get better familiarized" with its components

A day before *Purim*, and eight more are dead. In a coal-heated sealed room in Kfar Kassem, Amni Sarsur suffocated to death along with her sons, thirteen-year-old Mohammed and twelve- year-old Sameech. Twenty-seven-year old Ami Cohen was killed in an IDF operation in Bethlehem and will be buried in Netanya.

By fire, by gunshots, by human error and by targeted assassinations, they have perished, met their maker, returned to dust, lain to rest, passed on and left their mothers. Dov has not passed on, and is not dead or alive, he does not breathe and senses nothing, and I feel like an accomplice in some prolonged fraudulent deception.

In conversations with friends, their impatience is diluted with concern for me and the children. As if I had promised that his days were numbered and now have to justify the fact that his heart and kidneys are defying the laws of nature.

The merriment of Purim took over the ward by force. Young people holding Purim noisemakers hopped frantically around the beds and amongst the medical devices, singing and dancing in their foolish costumes, performing for an audience that cannot see, hear or react, and handed the relatives, who forced themselves to smile, handed tasteless hamantaschen wrapped in red cellophane. While the Purim revelry made its way to the hallways and the other wards, the war entered the ICU with grave patriotism. A new group of young people, volunteer students, tore off the cheap curtains, replacing them, with impressive skill, with sheets of plastic (100 microns thick, as stipulated by army regulations). They used rolls of polypropylene duct tape (thirty microns thick and five cm. wide), to seal the windows, taping the length, width and even going diagonally, closing off the airless, odor-ridden rooms. Ladders were folded up and dragged from room to room, and in a mix of concern and excitement the patients who were mobile offered the volunteers their Purim candy from the cellophane wrappers.

"The night arrangement" began. The bad smells and stale air drove me outside.

Dov, who cannot see or smell or hear, is nourished by the oxygen pumped into his lungs, and whether he lives or dies he will not take part in this war, nor in the *Purim* celebration or the 'Iron Wall' – which is the code name for the war that might take place. In fact, he hasn't fully taken part ever since 'Viper' (the code name for the missile attack on Israel during the Gulf War) and up to 'Operation Defensive Shield' and he will never know about the bulldozer that crushed Rachel Corrie to death in Rafah.

***

On this night, marking two weeks from the irreversible brain damage, I knew that it was only a matter of hours. I lingered beside his bed with my hand on his chest, feeling his heartbeat grow fast, as if it were reaching for the final goal indicated by the levels of potassium and creatinine in his blood -ten times the norm- and by the negligible amount of urine that his failing kidneys were to produce in their last effort.

My strength failed me, my nerves were frayed and all I wanted was to be alone. I stood there with my son and daughter, facing Dov's fluttering heart. The rate soared to 230 beats per minute and went down and up again crazily. The moments passed, but there was no way to gauge them. There were no comforting words but there wasn't suffering either, and no physical pain. Nor was there any of the comfort that can be offered or gained from being together. An insane, unnecessary war was being waged outside, far off, and Baghdad's red sky, the smoke and pillars of fire with the new title of "Shock and Awe," left us in a sealed room, soaked in sickening stench.

My daughter went home to her husband and daughter, Dan and his girlfriend retired to their apartment and as for me, having already said my goodbyes and paid my respects, my tears all dried up, I glanced at Dov's artificially respirated body and stepped outside, into air lacking freshness, and then to my home, and to my rest.

Before we said goodbye at the hospital, we deliberated. Racheli was adamant about having a secular burial, Dan wanted privacy and feared any publicity. Dov was not religious, did not believe in God or keep tradition. He was beyond being demonstrative about it, never protested and did not impose his choices upon others, ever-respectful of their freedom ot choose. I will never know for sure, but I believe that Dov would've wanted kaddish to be said over his grave, if only because his parents never had his say kaddish for them when they rose in the smoke of the crematorium. The accepted norms and customs, the compromise and even the banality, offered Dov a protective shield that set free the imagination and allowed for creativity, boldness and even sparks of idiosyncrasy. My strength was nary enough for explaining all of this on that cold night, as the signs of life disappeared from his body.

My children and I left Dov's flailing heart and an hour later we were called to return, just before midnight on Friday, to encounter his body covered with a sheet. I exposed his face, kissed his forehead and said goodbye to the warmth of his body, the warmth of his arms, and of his chest. I let my palm rest on what was a short while ago, the site of his stubbornly beating heart, and I let go. I wanted to run away from the room, from the dead body, the smells and the pounding of my own heart. Not to be there when the remainder of Dov's body heat evaporated, to run away and never stop.

He did not rest in peace, and the turmoil that I felt could not be discerned, for my eyes had long dried up, my mouth was parched, and I did not seek consolation. I sunk into myself, wrapped in pity, feeling as if I were tumbling down an incline with nothing to break the fall. At the end of the incline I felt the heat coming from Dov's limp hands, but he was sinking deeper and deeper and I had stopped, silently hovering in a nightly repose of stony emptiness.

Dov's death on the night between Friday and Saturday was an act of grace, leaving me an interim to function in slow motion and in delay mode, to mechanically go about all the necessary tasks between the time a body is covered over and transported to the morgue, and when it is buried.

On Saturday I got up with great difficulty; the difficulty of having everything that was anticipated and expected becoming a reality. I rummaged through the remains.

Frantically sort the past and the future, the bits of diamonds and dust, uprooting and planting, discarding and connecting.

We wrote a death notification ad for the Sunday papers. The opinion of the children and my Mother prevailed, and we did not write, as I wanted to, "please refrain from condolence visits." The mourning arranged itself, as if geared towards a brief mission with clear final objectives. People were somehow found for answering the phones, preparing the drinks, and muttering soft words of comfort in a low, barely audible voice.

Transitions

Glasses were loaded onto trays, the electric samovar was set out, as were the cookies, baked goods and freesias, my favorite flowers, which are beautiful in times of joy and in times of sorrow, white freesias in blue vases. All of the windows were opened, letting in the grey weather, clearing the house of the odors that had clung to it for years. Odors of urine, perspiration, air-fresheners and cologne, and those of dogs and the garlic and onions that were always fried for lunch, as well as the smell of old clothes and worn shoes, and I hysterically sort them out, as if I needed to leave for my own grave in the morning and never come back to see or touch them.

A merciful *Shabbat* followed, of the storm before the calm. Dov was taken to a room along with the other dead. The tubes were gently extracted from his body, he was washed and purified and he is still with us and not yet a memory, until the stars came out and the gloom of the mundane brought us back on the track that determines his burial place – the plot, block, grave number. After an argument with the children, we also resolved my own place of burial, in the upper level of the same grave. "After your 120th year" they said. And all the while Dov was still with me. Neither alive nor buried. He hadn't become a memory yet, he was there, a few streets away, not a warm body but a cold corpse, present in our world.

The funeral procession to block 30 in zone 1, row 21, grave number 3 (bottom level), was a struggle to fight back the tears and the weakness in my legs. One step after another step, endlessly.

Dov is carried on a gurney by strangers, and I am encircled by the people who loved him, the ones who love me and my children, until we reach the pit that had been dug up and the mound of crumbling earth, at which point I can't bear it any longer and avert my eyes as they slide the vulnerable, limp body into its designated place, as if it were being cruelly thrown out to predators. And then, since there was no coffin, the silence of the earth being piled up vigorously, the hoes and spades hard at work, like someone buried alive in an avalanche of snow or mud.

When I turned back again to look, my face streaming with tears, the pit had been covered and replaced by a reddish mound of earth, and there was even a temporary sign stuck in it. Dan read the words of the kaddish with emotion and a cantor nasally sang the prayer "El Malei Rachamim."

Many wreaths were placed on the grave, and the arrangement of narcissuses that I was holding was frozen in my hands as I move to place it next to that of our daughter. My own burial will be shorter. My coffin will be placed above Dov's and only the tombstone will be replaced by one bearing both our names.

People I know speak with hushed voices, shake my hands or hug me, my cousin Uzi reads a eulogy and a poem that leaves no eye dry. The croud disperses slowly and someone leads me away to a car and home as I feel faint and dizzy.

***

We stay on the muddy banks of the river, with Cerberus guarding the gates of Hades, and Dov, equipped with his wondrous deeds and his love as payment for Charon, the ferryman, for the crossing of the River Styx on his way to the underworld, begins edging

further away from the swampy, foul-smelling river bank, teeming with hatred and ridden with anger, where we will all remain until Charon concedes to take us over to the other side and Cerberos allows us to escape the refuse.

The house is full of friends and relatives and through their love the house is full of Dov. Stacks of photo albums and piles of pictures, unorganized and undated; Dov as a child with his family, at school in Munkacs, Dov with various young women –all strikingly beautiful– in Europe, in Jerusalem, in the military. Dov the Mossad agent, clad in a three-piece suit and a Burberry trench-coat in the alleys of London, Paris and Marseilles, leaning against a convertible sports car, a stray lock of hair on his forehead, a mysterious knowing smile on his lips. Dov the paratrooper, Dov with Arik and with Prime Ministers, Dov in Egypt, Dov with a microphone as IDF Spokesperson, Dov with Dan and Racheli and the entire family, in all the different periods. The Dov I knew and the Dov I didn't, and one or two recent photographs, a trip to Paris, to Italy, independence day celebrations, Dov with a feeding tube, fragile in his despair, with Racheli and Alma, a trace of a smile, the remnants of cognition. A newspaper photograph from the funeral: Dan saying *kaddish*.

And at night, when the house is emptied of people and forever empty of Dov, I am plagued by the recurring worms and maggots nightmare, and I try to fend off and remove the reptiles from his body; the shroud is crumbled and disintegrating and his eyes are gaping holes and I am beside myself, drenched in sweat, frightened.

Seven days, and during them a mixture of different pieces of a patchwork of memories, people who knew him and experienced them and those who didn't and asked about them. Friends of the children, family members, Edgardo's friends, friends from the wars and partners in peace. Blame and guilt hover in the room for seven days. Flashes of shame and regret from those who abandoned Dov and those who abandoned me, as they face their conscience before my wall of placating sadness, in that Dov's death was prolonged and his end was premature, and I adopt a closed-off, introspective type of mourning. Every day, until night falls and the comforting parts with the mourning. The voices fade away and an uninvited silence takes over.

For seven days the telegrams, letters and phone calls pile up, things are said and left unsaid, about him and me, to him and to me, and we sit and get up and provide food and drinks and weep and laugh and sort the visitors according to their levels of honesty and formality and, as mourners customarily do, we enumerate the people who didn't come by and didn't write, those we expected and those who surprised us by showing up and those were touching, causing us to tremble with emotion.

And I take care of the inventory like someone packing for a refugee about to flee, tossing out whatever isn't necessary after briefly running hands over it or shedding a tear. The clothes I gave away and donated. Fine clothes, all carefully selected and meticulously worn. Cashmere sweaters and tailored suits, shoes and sandals and, more recently, slippers. I remove Dov's rank symbols, Brigadier-General, from uniforms – which are clean and pressed – and take off the paratrooper's wings, the badges and medals from all the wars, and place them in a drawer next to a small gold custom-made Jeep that Dov gave me as a gift when we married, a playful reference to the day we met on a dusty Jeep right before the war broke out in 1967.

There are watches with bold, easy to read numbers – long ago he had given Racheli the Rolex I got him when we married – and reading glasses, sunglasses, speech and hearing aids that no one has any use for. It feels uncomfortable to throw away a dead person's glasses, or fairly new dentures, and I pack everything up carefully and throw them out discreetly. X-rays, medical records, brain MRIs, the black damaged material, the prescriptions and leftover drugs, cartons of the nutritious supplement that had replaced meals of pasta and spicy Szechuan sauces. Bandages, ointments, IV bags, thickeners, adult diapers still in their boxes. I donate whatever is sealed in its package to the clinic, for other patients to use. In a modest drawer there are the items that have enabled Dov to cross the Styx. I saved the red paratrooper berets that belonged to Dov and his younger brother Zvi, and gave the gold Jeep to Alma for her second birthday.

I also kept the pens that he loved, the books in Czech and in Russian, countless photographs, letters that he wrote to me and files that could be of interest to our children someday – or will yellow and be forgotten.

I sink low and then raise my spirits, grow weak and then force myself to be strong, run away and come back to myself, for his slow death had kept me company, it was a comforting calling, giving purpose to my days and my nights.

I did not manage to stop the end of the journey, nor could I postpone it. I wove and spun during the day and watched my work unravel at night, and I returned to a hopeless fabric, the horizon distant.

> Keep Ithaka always in your mind
> Arriving there is what you are destined for
> But not hurry the journey at all
> Better if it lasts for years
> Ithaka gave you the marvelous journey
> Without her you would not have set out
> She has nothing left to give you now.[19]

Ithaka no longer has anything to give me and this journey has ended. The threads that were woven and undone, and later rewoven, have been discarded, they are unwanted and I must feel my way through to other paths. The marble tombstone in the cemetery is engraved with bronze lettering that reads:

---

19 C.P. Cavafy, "Ithaka." Translated by Edmund Keeley/Philip Sherrard.

Yael Dayan

Brigadier-General Dov Sion Son
of Rachel and David Steiger
1920-2003
Beloved, Friend, and Father to the End of Time

From the Ministry of Interior and the IDF I got a new identity. The "personal status" on my identification card now reads "widow". I am bothered by the passiveness of the word. Married, divorced - words that indicate partnership , decision-taking. "Widow"– something that happened to me when the struggle for Dov's life ended. In the "Information Leaflet for Widows of IDF Pensioners" there are details of the survivor's allowance and the discount benefits to which I am entitled as a widow for everything from cultural events, vacations and entertainment, to loans and nursing homes.

I conduct myself slowly. The ache in my leg has gotten worse and I try all kinds of medication and pain killer injections. I need recovery time in order to settle myself into this new loneliness.

The warmth in which I enveloped Dov now shines out of me, providing a patient kind of quality to my relationships with my friends and my children, and it then dissolves and turns, for them, into embarrassing excess. The umbilical cord of the years of Dov's illness, which once constituted atonement and closeness, transforms itself at the very end into a suffocating noose– and is severed.

I need time for the soul's anguish. At the market, instead of a crate of oranges, I select two or three items of fruit of every kind. Instead of a loaf of bread, I buy a roll or two, as befitting aging windows who have fewer mouths to feed and who harbor a fear of any excess or leftovers.

My children and I do not operate according to the principle of connecting vessels.

They are afraid I might ask for reparations or something in return when my sheltering wings become a burden.

They are concerned about my weight loss and the withered, wrinkled flesh of my arms and thighs, the white roots in my hair, the protruding veins on the backs of my hands, and the tears pooling in the corners of my eyes. I part with them, each going their own way, and a thread of love, lighter than air and impossible to sever, is cast from me to them. I ask, temporarily, to have a moment of grace for myself. Only temporarily for soon we set-up a new equilibrium, my children accepting me as their single parent adjusting to a new set of rules.

> My thoughts, soft as down, cushion me comfortably
> I've found a very simple method,
> not so much as a foot-breadth on land and not flying, either—
> hovering at a low altitude. [20]

---

20 Dahlia Ravikovitch "Hovering at a Low Altitude" Translated by Chana Bloch and Chana Kronfeld

Chapter 12

The locked room. I have a history.

The year began with a series of depressing and frustrating events – Yom Kippur, the anniversary of father's death, the memorial of Rabin's assassination, and for the first time in two decades, I was not running for an elective office.

The bad streak continued with the unexpected death of a friend. He had been diagnosed with metastatic cancer and would likely suffer a great deal of pain when he came to seek my advice about ending his life. Suicide is perhaps the only freedom we have between birth and death. To offer advice and interfere with such a profound liberty is impossible. I could not fulfil his request.

He petitioned for, and was granted euthanasia and it was not because he lost control or went insane. The decision is entirely in our own hands – when the line should be severed. In which state we choose to withdraw and end the circle, which is not really a circle but a dotted line with a beginning and an end to it.

He made a brave, conscious decision, weighing his accomplishments against the suffering that awaited him, and he chose the moment to make the final cut. Beyond that point, the future in store for him had nothing of quality, nothing noble or agreeable to it. He chose not to postpone the decision and mark the ending point for what body and spirit can endure rather than begin a pointless struggle for each additional day. That is how I regarded it. Was it courage, or fear of the impending future?

You put yourself in his position. You think of Aharona and her peaceful, beautiful death when medicine had nothing more to offer. Will you know when you are no longer possible? WIll you put aside all of the desires, hopes and fears and let the freedom of the decision prevail and have the truest, best moment of liberty in your life? You don't want to reach the point of undignified, inhumane physical suffering. Your main fear is losing sanity and lucidity, not being aware of your experiences. You dread the thought that people will ask "how is she" and be answered by a vague wave of the hand, expressing despair, defining you as unsound.

Yael Dayan

You are frightened by the in-between state. An error in navigation, forgetting names and contexts; you fear that pre-dementia will prevent you from grasping the gravity of the situation, or won't allow ample time for recognizing the moment when you still will be able to say, "This is not how I want to live. Let me say goodbye."

Why is it easier for you to write death than to write life? The death of your father gave rise to a book, and the urge to express yourself in words reawakened towards the end of Dov's life, when he was no longer the center of your life and could not communicate his awareness of you. Perhaps because there is no way out, there is no longer someone to listen or share experiences, no heart to understand; it is the absolute form of loneliness that death imposes. You grit your teeth and open the notebook. You could not discuss the smell of urine and feces, the repulsive concoction that was shoved into a hole in his stomach and digestive system, you could not mention the desire to run away and the love that held you back, the signs of doubt that shook your entire foundation, and you wrote.

The pages were always given to Dahlia to read, dear Dahlia whom you admired and who was the most honest of them all. Until tragedy struck, and Dahlia died. After delivering her eulogy and guiltily taking on a brave silence, you stopped writing.

Dahlia was an ethereal presence to you, a fairy, scattering her black diamonds, cracking open chasms deep within you, ones that had no possibility of consolation. You were addicted to the mercurial spirit of her life and even her death did not bring about a release and the pages that she read were filed away, waiting for a sign.

With her death, the seven, or some say nine, muses and Apollo that had called upon you day and night, were replaced with the Moirae sisters, the three sisters of fate. Clotho– the weaver of the thread of life, Lachesis– the measurer of thread, and Atropos– the cutter of thread.

A liturgical poem, piut, called "Unetanneh Tokef" was discovered in the 'Cairo Geniza'. It is a poem of reckoning, self-examination and remorse, and most of all, it is a recognition of the insignificance of human beings. While beautifully written, it exudes an impossible form of faith, complete diminishment in the face of a divine higher power, compared to God we are likened to "a broken shard, withering grass, a fading flower, a passing shade, a dissipating cloud, a blowing wind, flying dust, and a fleeting dream." [21] The Hebrew imagery is drawn from nature and the use of verbs is precise: exalted, withering, fading, passing, flying, fleeting – all aimed to create a detailed, accurate picture of the transient, the meaninglessness of a "now" which has no forever.

It is not a malicious description, nor is it insulting or humiliating, but rather a realistic, almost beautiful, reminder of our nullity, which is not absolute, but relative – in comparison with the creator.

When the shofar will blow and the sound will break through all of the dividers, we will promise the creator of the universe our loyalty to the purpose of our life on earth.

Once again, the tired old question of a predestined, deterministic purpose arises– providence, duplicating genes to infinity, preserving the genus and species of worms, lizards, maggots and primates, apes and Homo erectus. We are all here for a reason

21 From the piut "Unetanneh Tokef".

100

and we are propelled towards it, moving on the conveyor belt with the various props, tools, hardships and marvels of joy that are added and taken away from the journey.

My friend wanted to get off the conveyor belt. He was my age, handsome and refined; he was happy in his personal life amongst family and friends but his public persona was filled with indignation – angry about our nation's present state and apprehensive about its future. He accepted the fact that the goals would never be reached and nevertheless insisted on carrying on the path of morality and justice, which once was the accepted norm and the road of the founding fathers until it was brutally severed by the murder in the square. He fought against the decay that rose up in a cloud of steam and settled across the land, spreading with messianic drunkenness, reaching out to seize the land of others. He fought against those poisoned by corruption who uprooted olive trees and sowed evil, and he died with the faith that we would continue on the same path even without bearing witness to his suffering. He had had enough of his future life and perhaps he tired of us as well.

My body is in turmoil due to my mood. The hunger for oxygen halts all activity and sends spasms of pain from my back down to my hips and knees, reaching all the way to my feet and toes. I need oxygen to settle my heart. I can sense the hatred, which is bottomless, as it overpowers, crushes, dances in the blood, and I listen to my heart pounding and my lungs exhaling, thirsty for more and more air.

I am not well these days. I feel ungrateful. Despite the loneliness, I am independent; I am blessed with a bright apartment and blossoming plants, I take part in efforts to do good, to promote progress and make a positive impact, however futile those attempts may be. I do no harm, I harbor no hatred or desire for revenge, and I still gather bits and pieces of knowledge and remain enthusiastic about books, enjoy the theater and new discoveries; I share everything I have with my grandchildren, as their parents are engrossed in their own lives and their daily toil and I am marginal in their lives, trying to maintain boundaries and not become a bother or a burden.

If there is love, it isn't a dependent kind, and the children's criticism and judgement is one-sided; I suppress my comments and reactions as much as I can, confining them to the chambers of the heart, there too, the oxygen supply is low. I have no doubt in my heart that their impatient love will dwindle in time.

I tread with caution, so as not to extinguish it prematurely.

Finally Autumn. The weather is wonderful; the parakeets are shrieking, drowning out the chirps of the honey suckers, piercing the clouds that cover the sky. The blue jacaranda has shed its glorious purple blossoms but remains cloaked in lush green foliage. The herbs in the window boxes are flourishing, bearing seeds and buds. Soon they will wilt in the heavy rains ,if they come.

The lavender plants burst forth in bundles, overflowing in the planters and swaying in the wind and beside them bloom gigantic yellow hibiscus and allamanda flowers. I am gathering up the remains of a decade of work; I want to pass on my heritage to the hands and heart that will nurture everything and everybody who need an open ear and a caressing attention and will offer supporting and reprimanding if need be.

Final trickles of love and respect come my way– handshakes and farewell kisses– with no festivities, no distinguishing marks separating them from other people's yesterdays, today's and tomorrows. New employee badges will be issued, with new photos, a new password for the computer and my license plate number will be deleted from the list that automatically opens the parking lot gate. That too is a status symbol.

I gather my personal items, the photos and newspaper cuts. Faded, yellowing clippings have now been replaced by computer scanned printouts, and the articles and interviews have spawned talkbacks – a new creature, the offspring of hate letters and graffiti, an inarticulate weapon, able to remain nameless in the gutter.

What fans the flames of abuse and sparks such intense disgust and hatred in people I have never met? People who would write the following words in response to an article about a surgery I underwent:

She needs a lobotomy...worn out old hag...oh, poor thing, the prima donna had a bit of pain...when will we finally be rid of her? wheeen?...one of the most hypocritical and repulsing women in the history of politics...she achieved everything because she has the right connections….Yael had a treacherous father, a crazy friend, a druggie-brother and an anti-Israeli agenda, she shouldn't be babbling...etc.etc.

A few weeks later, as a farewell gift for ending my term in the municipality, I got a re-run of the same insults, along with suggestions for a new career:

I hear that Hizballah is looking for a Hebrew-speaker...yalla retire already, no one can stand you...

why don't you let the infiltrators [asylum seekers] stay at your house you despicable old woman, go join your ancestors, you repulsive old woman…

You know that the paper accepts everything, and there are no limits to what can be printed. You manage to restrain the urge to respond, but you cannot help read the words, reflecting on the tremendous difference between the warmth, approval and the admiration that you receive on one hand– and the wishes for your death and destruction on the other. How different are you from the pathetic character that they describe; a worn out old hag, unappealing, devoid of substance, hypocritical, despised? And why can't you carry on with pride and confidence, casting off the insulting words and holding your head high, staying on your path, on your terms? Perhaps you aren't sure of your destination? Just as when Alice in Wonderland asks the Cheshire Cat whether to turn right or left, and he answers "that depends on where you want to go".

Where do you want to go?

No one can share the question with you or answer it ,for you are alone in every crossroad.

And in the seventy-fourth year of your life, the only people you can turn to are no longer alive. Your father, Dahlia, Dov. Your children have answers, but they do not address your questions and do not ease your anxieties. They'd rather state their own.

What they think is best for you, what they consider proper, dignified, worthy of you. Things you should or shouldn't do, how to present yourself, what to say and when to say it. They offer their advice in good faith, protecting themselves as well, lest you do something that would embarrass, disappoint or reflect poorly on them, lest it encroaches on their privacy, which they have worked so hard to protect, whereas you have abandoned and forfeited your own. I resume my naïve and curious wandering of the mind.

Darwinian evolution and the evolution of culture. I try to look beyond the horizon and come to terms with death and the fact that life is over "in a blink of an eye". I am amazed at the time –approximately a million years- that spanned between the development of the ability to stand up and walk on two legs and the large size of the brain of modern man. The traditional belief favoring man's superiority links brain size with human progress. The view fostered arguments such as the inferior status of women because their brains are smaller than men's, and the racist pseudoscience of phrenology. However, later research refuted the belief in the precedence of brain size, attributing the major breakthroughs in development of mankind from the Hominids and the Chimpanzees to the erect posture and the development of two-legged locomotion.

Prehistoric man in his upright form, with his erect posture and small brain (a third smaller than that of modern man) developed, gained skills and used tools for approximately four million years before the next modification came about– the enlargement of the brain.

Bipedal mode was a fundamental anatomical change and after a while it affected the anatomy of the cerebrum. For four million years, our ancestors, including Lucy, the hominid, walked upright, on two legs, and carried within their small heads, behind their small jaws, a fairly small brain. In the course of a million years, the brain tripled in size and brought the large brained Homo erectus to its current state. And at this point, we leave Darwin to focus on the cultural evolution that took place in giant leaps as man started on a course of discoveries and inventions, beliefs and refutations, developing thought, reason and the ability to learn, teach, draw conclusions and inferences, observe, cultivate, reconstruct, create and even duplicate. Most likely ourselves as well. At times, my preoccupation with fate, free will, life and death is obsessive.

In the meantime, I take in the physical changes in my life. I pack up the office, sorting the items, moving some of them home, deliberating about several issues that I remain responsible for and changing my business cards. I order the new ones at the old and slow printer's shop across the street, along with new stationery and postcard-size papers to serve as thank-you notes or best wishes as well as words of condolences. thank you notes.

I return to my roots. Name, address and phone number, without a logo or title. The way I used to be more than twenty years ago, before the elections and the Knesset. I only add my email and mobile phone number– information that progress necessitates. regular font. They lack the humiliating prefix of "former". Former Knesset Member, former Deputy Mayor, former Chair of the City Council. I certainly have no need for a retrospective and my hand still trembles at the sight of the most meaningful box that is ticked on various forms such as my id card, which is marked "widow".

I have a history. When I want to experience it, I enter the locked room. In that space, I can revisit the past and all of its exciting and terrifying moments with the safety of knowing it can never be revived or changed, and that I need not erase it.

I slide into another period of time, to another "me", caught in a captivating, sensual love affair across the ocean with a man who broke off the relation when he chose the love of a man over mine.

Then I relive the indulgent, sensuous European courtship that lasted for several years and spanned different countries, languages and flavors; my love was playful and coy and he was unable to commit to a future together, which suited me well at the time.

Another unsuccessful affair ended on the verge of violence and I had to flee to the other end of the world. The room also contains many of the frivolous delights the world has to offer.

An Alfa-Romeo convertible; the hydraulic suspension Citroen, well- suited for the dirt roads of Crete while shooting Zorba the Greek; jewelry that I have long stopped wearing; and a string of my failures that have been documented. A speech I gave at the Knesset when Barak (Prime Minister at the time) did not nominate me as a Minister in his government, certificates for the various training courses I enrolled in – corporate director, mediator, mediator for matrimonial law, my application for the position of public representative at the Labor Court and the applications and references for a variety of ambassador posts. I sought to explore other tracks that corresponded with my own, expanded my horizons and were beneficial, yet I only succeeded when the public was the one casting the ballot.

Did I overestimate myself? Aim higher than my capabilities? The musings weren't ones I wanted to share.

In my history I have aspirations that cannot be met. "This life is too short for our souls" said Goethe, the soul grows stronger, erupts, yearns and imagines, only to discover that we are shrinking, being consumed; that there is only one act in the play that our soul has written and our time is up.

I emerge from the cluttered room, reentering real life with the strong desire to run away, to flee from myself, from the heaviness, to exist in a different kind of air.

I want to press a magic button and find myself in another place. Without any goodbyes or warm welcomes, without packing, purchasing ticketing and arriving on time for the departure of a plane, a ship or a train, without carrying any luggage, documents, maps or provisions. Free, the way I used to be.

Chapter 13

A grandmother, 75. Revisiting the world.
The clenched fist is now trembling fingers.

I have to get away in order to breathe. I long for the ocean, not the sandy beach, seashells, children laughing or curvy young women giving themselves up to the sun. I long for an ocean that doesn't have gentle undulations, I long for an ocean that contains the abyss, that emits the thunderous sound of thousands of swollen-bellied beasts as they turn over onto their backs, a natural roar that could only be produced far from shore, in the dark of night.

I took the small portable oxygen generator, my cane and the larger oxygen generator for nightly use. I packed a suitcase with books and blank paper, some cosmetics and comfortable clothes, and made my way to Ben-Gurion Airport where I boarded a plane to Rome. Then I took the shuttle to Civitavecchia and went up to the ninth floor of the large ship, entering a spacious cabin complete with a private balcony.

I don't like swimming in rough waters. I am even afraid of the waves that break on the shore. I have an early childhood memory of being swept beneath a wave; I swallowed salt water and the terrifying sensation lingered long after I was pulled out. But I am drawn to it; we all originate in the ocean, and we are borne on the breaking waves. I can sense the ebb and flow, the velocity, the moisture absorbed by the sand, and the fear of being swallowed up by the abyss.

The cabin was comfortable. I unpacked my suitcase and watched the shore receding, waiting for the special kind of darkness in which the ocean and the sky become indistinguishable. As the lights of Italy grew distant, we became engulfed in darkness, not a star could be seen in the sky and I was content. I ventured out for dinner. The ship was swaying gently, pleasantly. I sat down at the single table I had reserved, the oxygen tank ensured I would be served first.

"Which language?" asked the waiter wearing a suit and tie.

"It doesn't matter," I responded. I can get by in several languages when shopping and eating out.

I listened patiently as he described the specials and then opted for something light, adding a glass of wine to the order. I pulled out my book, the first of four I brought along for the week.

After dinner I went out for a walk on the deck. It was cool, and I forced myself to cover the entire length of the deck, wrapped in a warm scarf I picked up in St.Petersburg. My mother– I bought her one too– mentioned that the scarves knit from yak wool only came from young yaks, which have the best quality wool. Elderly couples, pairs of women or an occasional lone man were also out surveying the deck and they greeted me as we passed each other. I replied but made no attempt to communicate any further. It wasn't necessary.

On one side of the ship you could see lights flickering the distance, or the glimmer of a cautioning lighthouse beam. The oxygen and pain in my hips were limiting, and I relied heavily on the cane, aware of the noise coming from the fifth floor where the casinos, restaurants and cafes were located; an entire city was cradled below, bustling in a hodgepodge of languages and dialects: Russian, Japanese, loud grating American and heavily accented, proper English.

There were also several Hebrew speakers onboard and I accidentally overheard:

"I think I saw Yael Dayan with an oxygen tube in her nose." "I thought it was her too, but Yael Dayan is younger."

I drank in the salty air with a faint smile of relief. All in all, I had it good on the upper deck, suspended between the ocean and the sky, I had no need to arrive at a particular destination nor would I find it there, even if I knew what it was.

We docked in Naples and I was transported back in time almost six decades ago, to my first trip to Europe, which was also my first experience abroad. I sailed aboard a "Zim" passenger ship accompanied by my maternal grandmother, Rachel. Her Peugeot was parked in the belly of the ship. We were greeted by the sight of the Vesuvius, with its two protruding humps, and encountered the cracked city of Naples, the narrow alleyways and the paint peeling on the houses.

I was insatiable. The fruits in the marketplace, the peaches and apples tasted nothing like the ones growing on our trees back home. The traffic, the cars, motorbikes, the noise, the musical language and the scents bore no resemblance to anything I had experienced in Tel Aviv or Haifa. Everything overwhelmed me with confusing sensuality.

My grandmother remained composed in the midst of this dumbfounding encounter. She was well-groomed, spoke several languages and was able to assign things their proper place and value; she wasn't over-excited and perhaps could not understand the experience of an awkward country girl who lost her footing as soon as she stepped out of her small, limited world.

We sailed from Naples to Marseilles and began a long and eventful journey, as she drove on stunning roads that predated the freeways, tunnels and bridges. We covered the length of France, passing through Belgium, Holland and Germany before reaching Stockholm, Oslo and the Bergen Port in the North Sea, where we boarded another ship, this time sailing in wild, stormy waters to Newcastle where we docked and took the car to London. We arrived in London after weeks of travel; I had been tossed about and managed to regain a sense of calm and emerge with newfound maturity. I had experienced the world's absurdity and its hardships, I witnessed Europe post WWII, a continent that had yet to recover, whose wounds were still open. I felt as if I had tasted both the honey and the stale black bread. In London, Grandma Rachel rented me a room in an apartment belonging to a family friend and found me a part-time job as a translator for a Jewish newspaper. Then she went on her way, leaving me there. Our journey, which began at the Piazza Garibaldi ended on Fleet Street had brought about a change within me, revealing a great deal that I still could not define. I felt ready for independence, I wanted to go out into the world and accomplish things, to make my own mistakes and I was prepared to take on responsibility.

I was just shy of my seventeenth birthday, pretty, unsophisticated, wobbling on my low heels, curious and eager, and I had an endless passion for knowledge – even to the point of peril.

Fifty-five years later, I headed to the beach, deliberately going slow. After the platform emptied of all of the bus tours, I flagged down a taxi and visited the Piazza Garibaldi. From the Piazza I made my way through the ancient city and reached the Piazza San- Domenico-Maggiore. Gothic churches, an obelisk in the square, coffee and pizza. I could still sense the atmosphere of post-war Europe. The dirt, the meaninglessness, the laundry hanging across the narrow streets, the small shops and makeshift stalls, the fading red-pink paint and the volcano that loomed above it all, which gave a sense of permanence in an atmosphere of transience and haste. Taking my cue from Malaparte, I thought of the defeat of the victors in the war. [22] "Skin" and "Kaputt" had influenced me in my youth. I thought of the fascists that had been transformed and fought Mussolini and Hitler, witnessing the horror of the victors and of those defeated, the surrealism of the pre-peace era and Italy's decline.

Dov was there towards the end of the war. He joined forces with the British Army during the invasion. Arriving in Sicily, he watched as American innocence met with British punctiliousness and together they witnessed the evil crumbling around them.

Wild, atrocious, rumors were circulating and Dov drove out to the place that had been his home in search of his mother and father. He was confronted with orphanhood and forced to begin another life.

I returned to my cabin, leaving behind the memories that stopped by for a visit. The ship passed the coast of Sorrento, Amalfi, Capri– places I was loved and loved in, bays of peace, triumphs of romantic beauty. The beach at Positano, or Ravello, where the houses hang on cliffs above the blue of the ocean. It is hard not to fall in love with them as decor, to refuse being courted as the body succumbs and cries out for romance I found it impossible to break off a love affair there, or part for good.

But not anymore. I am grateful for the past, for what I used to be and for everything I managed to soak up, pleasant enough to provide cushioning for atrophying cells.

---

22 Curzio Malaparte, an Italian author and journalist.

Yael Dayan

Aeolus, the Greek god of the wind, spared those suffering from sea sickness, and the ocean named after him was calm. I traveled the volcanic islands that Odysseus sailed, from Lipari to Stromboli, disappointed by the smoothness of the waves. I was expecting the bow of the ship to point high and low on the horizon and I wanted to hear the whoosh of the waters rushing by the stern, but this time the ship did not rock or sway. The lighthouses glimmered; illuminating the course of the cruise as we calmly sailed from Messina and Sicily to Sardinia.

The sky was bright on the third night of the cruise, and from my balcony I could make out all of the stars and constellations, arranged exactly the way I studied and later taught them to my children. Cassiopeia and Orion, the North Star– The Big Dipper, which was the pretext for an embrace with my first steady boyfriend. We both had our eyes fixed at the sky, betting on "who will be first to find the Big Dipper," while sprawled out on a rock in The Valley of the Cross on a star-studded night in the fresh spring air of Jerusalem. A first kiss.

I looked up at the sky, they were all there apart from the Crux constellation The Southern Cross, which belongs to another sky, and another voyage.

We docked at Cagliari, Sardinia and I took my time before heading down to the port. I sat on the balcony, watching the seagulls as they circled around me.

The seagull is an accurate bird. From above, its wings appear slanted or broken. And when it soars overhead, alone or in a flock, its plumage looks like it was taken apart and then glued back together, resembling a stuffed animal. When the ship starts to move, the seagulls focus on their dives and ascents. But the rest of the time they act like peaceful retirees taking a day trip rather than hungry animals after their prey. Birds bear likeness to flowers and the seagull resembles a gladiola or a white calla lily.

Cagliari was the last Italian city on the itinerary, and the cruise now headed for the oceans and cities of Spain. The name "Sardinia" brought me back to *The Sardinian Drummer Boy, The "Little Hero of Lombardy* and *The Little Patriot of Padua*.

I remember reading the words on the page when I was a little girl and the tears I shed over the patriotic songs of sacrifice and heroic battle. The stories were unlike any others I read; they differed from the children's stories in Frontiersmen of Israel, the tales of the revolt of the Maccabees or the bravery of Josef Trumpeldor, nor were they similar to the stories of "Nili" the Jewish underground espionage network that aided the United Kingdom during WWI, or the "Absolutely Absolute Secret Group" (*Hasamba* in Hebrew) the popular series of children's adventure novels.

Nowadays, the stories in *The Heart* would likely be shelved.[23] They describe a form of love for their country that precedes the love of mankind and depicts children sacrificing themselves for the sake of Italy's unity. We have already been well schooled in patriotic nationalism with brown uniforms.

It was a warm autumn in Sardinia, and when I finally stepped off of the ship, I noticed that the trees were still green and had not yet shed their leaves. As in Tel Aviv, there were a few final clusters of purple flowers on the blue jacaranda, which had

---

23 Edmondo De Amicis, *The Heart*

stained the ground all through summer, and the boulevard boasted shade-giving ficus trees and Washingtonia palms, just like home. The taxi dropped me off at the entrance to one of the large department stores. I walked laboriously, aided by the cane, the portable oxygen device slung over my shoulder. I was on my way to perform the inevitable chore that is part of every trip I take– buying presents.

My sole motivation for this joyless, exhausting task is the expressions on the faces of my grandchildren when they open their gifts and a little dream comes true for each one of them, whether it's a T-Rex dinosaur or the new One Direction CD. I hate shopping, except for food and books. Nowadays the stores in Israel stock the items that once carried the allure of travel. They may be expensive but they're available, unlike the past when gifts from foreign lands were proof that there was a whole other world outside of our own, where the borders were sealed and the Tzena austerity measures were firmly in place.

Everything that came from other countries was considered a luxury. I could picture myself as a heroine from one of my books, walking proudly, wearing rustling taffeta gowns and wide brimmed hats that shrouded my mysterious eyes.

Delicate and romantic little gifts from abroad, daintily wrapped and tied with ribbons, were signs of the magnificent tales that lay hidden within their folds.

I was shopping for presents in Sardinia, going up and down the escalator, moving through the aisles, searching for the correct sizes and the right items to suit everyone's tastes. I needed something for my mother and something for my daughter and each one of the grandchildren. I felt tired and began to get dizzy until I finally had to lean against one of the shelves, dropping the shopping bag in desperation. Someone brought me a glass of water and a chair. I wasn't ashamed, I was angry at myself for getting caught in such a helpless situation. The battery in the portable oxygen generator had run out and I used an inhaler that I keep in my bag to draw long breaths of air. I slowly regained my bearings, and in Italian, asked for help getting to a taxi.

It is hard for me to acknowledge my limitations. I am not prepared to accept the finish line, slow down or narrow my horizons. I am not content to sit back and watch things pass me by. I cannot stay out of the current.

I returned to my cabin with the oxygen and a newfound recognition of my dependence on it. A phone call from home. "Yes, wonderful, I feel great, everything is fine. I was ashore, I picked up a few gifts for the children...no, it's not difficult at all, the weather is nice, kisses…"

With no witnesses around, I have no need to pretend. I relaxed, smoothing out the wrinkled remainders of the fear, the hunger for air and shortness of breath. I stood up and attempted to walk without the oxygen. I failed again. Slowly, I told myself, go slower.

I am ashamed of the misleading impression that I am handling my situation well and coping "heroically." I know that I am merely concealing my disability. When alone, I restore my speech and breath pattern and only then, as if I still had the strength, do I slowly set out to the next resting place.

Yael Dayan

Pretense gives me a sense of security because I require vitality even if it is not real. It allows me to walk with a sure step, to banish the tremor from my voice and the dryness from my throat. I examine myself the way I want to be seen to others, in particular my grandchildren and close friends. I have set the stage elaborately, disguising reality, succeeding in my role.

Sometimes I am too successful and my daughter says that maybe I am just "pretending to be sick, because you can manage just fine when you want to." I don't argue with her. But alone I am naked. My respiratory system has been reduced to two lead balloons with no discernable cycle of inflation and deflation. Worthless.

I find myself needing the wheelchair more often, the oxygen generator can only run as long as its battery and I need to make a choice: either walking a few meters with the cumbersome oxygen, tiring quickly and suffering from pain in my legs, or sitting in a wheelchair without being dependant on the oxygen battery, or at least conserving it.

It's still hard for me to adjust to the image created by the combination of the wheelchair and the oxygen generator, tubes in my nostrils and all.

The following day I skipped the shore and stayed in my cabin, sitting on the balcony and watching the seagulls and the ships docking at Palma de Mallorca. I had been there before, there was no need to test my capabilities.

I smiled to myself as I remembered Grandfather Shmuel, my father's father. He was much more of a seafarer than me; he sailed in order to see the world and study its beautiful artifacts, and he recorded it all in a journal where he challenged the very fact of indulging in the luxury of a cruise.

In the early sixties he went on two cruises. His first was aboard the 'Jerusalem' and the second toured the coast aboard the 'Shalom'. He wrote a journal chronicling his travels and a great deal of it is dedicated to the deliberations that preceded his trips. He wrote that a cruise is nothing more than "sheer idleness. Wasting money abroad," that it negates "moral imperatives such as prudence and efficiency," and that "your society, the one that you represent, is correct to shun such extravagances." But the day after writing those lines he boarded the ship, accompanied by his second wife Yona. He continued to record his thoughts even when they disembarked and took a tour of the port cities. Grandpa Shmuel also drew comparisons between farming at home and his impressions of the agriculture while travelling by bus from Switzerland to France: "Vast fields, bundles of grain, very little industrialization.

The field crops are divided into small plots–heavy rain. How do they harvest the wet grain?' He was awestruck at the sight of the castles and works of art and he toured Versailles plagued by the question: "Where did all of this wealth come from? Looting, exploitation and slavery– all for the sake of the pleasures of the privileged."

He brought me and all his grandchildren small plaster replicas of Socrates and Plato as presents. In his final years he devoted himself to reading the Greek philosophers, trying to make up for his education, which he felt was lacking.

I come from Nahalal, which has no ocean, from the landlocked Jerusalem of the British Mandate, and from Tel Aviv, where the waves are low.

Transitions

The hidden secrets of the sea seemed to be an attainable challenge. The early explorers didn't merely discover new shores; they also discovered themselves. The ocean was a man's world, ambition and camaraderie were the driving forces behind its exploration. The women were Penelope, Helena and the Sirens. The sea, its dark depths and infinite horizon featured prominently in the adventure stories I read, which enthralled me and sparked my imagination. I read the translated editions of Verne's *In Search of the Castaways, The Mysterious Island, Twenty Thousand Leagues Under the Sea* and enjoyed books such as *Moby Dick, The Old Man and the Sea* and *Endurance: Shackleton's Incredible Voyage.* The books also enriched my knowledge of geography, geology and fostered a sense of wild adventure and reliance on the human spirit.

I accepted as a matter of course the fact that all of the characters I admired were men, and that the kind of determination and steadfast courage they displayed was exclusive to them. I never dreamt that someday I would fight for women's rights in the IDF, championing equality so women could become pilots and sailors.

It was the last night at sea before we docked in Barcelona and flew back home. I gathered my belongings, the devices that support my breathing and all of the chargers, the handwritten pages and the presents for the children. I am not sure that I will have the strength to take another cruise on my own. I am also not ready to anchor at home permanently. Lately I have the urge to enter the locked room and examine its hidden secrets, perhaps traces of the past can rekindle the spark that has been extinguished.

Autumn is brief in Tel Aviv. A welcome but deceptive guest. The deciduous climbers do not turn yellow, and as soon as the sun sets, the air becomes crisp and my bright apartment is overrun by shadows. The few clouds lift my mood and scatter the heavy feelings that come with the heat waves and the humidity.

I close the windows and roll up the blind to ease the gloom of the cold, dark space. The city glitters as the dispersed high-rises are all lit up, dispelling some of the loneliness imparted by the changing of the seasons that no longer has romance to go with it. "You'll have time for yourself now. You can do anything you want."

As if I still had my whole life ahead of me. I no longer have an office or a job or any obligations and I am not required to respond to anyone or lend my support, propose initiatives and vote for or against them.

You do not anticipate any change for the better. You feel trapped, both within a body that cannot function properly and inside your pleasant apartment. You have no desire to participate in the events taking place outside. The calendar on your desk and the daily planner in your purse are mostly empty. The doctor's appointments and checkups you have scheduled are spaced weeks apart; there is a mammography, another one for mother, a bone-density scan, pulmonary lung function tests and an appointment at a rheumatology clinic for injections because the pain in your joints, like the volume of your lungs, cannot be cured, it just gets progressively worse.

When asked to rate the pain on a scale of one to ten you do not tell the truth, either underrating it when you feel a sudden burst of hopeful energy and want to please your physician; or overrating it when all of the external pressures close in on you, clouding your vision and feeding yourself pity.

Every week you drive the children to their afterschool activities. You are not the only one to volunteer. You pick them up whenever you can, bringing them back to your apartment or dropping them off at ballet, volleyball, piano or guitar lessons and once in a while you make the effort and take them home, slowly, painfully climbing the stairs, but only on special occasions.

My caretaker's days off are marked on the calendar, Wednesdays and weekends to attend Mass. On my calendar there are also Opening nights of theatres ,book-launching events and scientific lectures.

There is something for the soul and something for the brain.

Both are thirsty for what remains out of reach, and you make due with compromises. You know that you are replaceable. As the grandchildren grow older, they will sail off in their own directions, briefly stopping to find comfort in the safety of your love, which will always be greater than the love they have for you.

The same thing happened with the children. According to Dahlia:

> "And do we love our children?
> Sometimes we love our children, and even that
> mostly in a limited way
> as a citrus tree loves an orange.
> Beyond that, a whole range of misunderstandings
> greedily eat away at real love." [24]

You think it is the other way around. Sometimes your children love you, as an orange loves a citrus tree. Your grandchildren now occupy the space in your hollow lap that once held the children; it is filled with love for them and that too will pass. The weary head of a child will no longer seek out the crook of your arm or the comfort of your lap, he will be satisfied with a quick kiss as he bends down to offer you the top of his head or his cheek before quickly moving on.

Grandchildren have always been longed for, and when life spans were shorter, most grandparents died before they could see their children become grandparents themselves. Young children do not like wrinkled skin or bulging veins. They are slightly scared of the great-grandmother who demands a hug and a kiss. My mother loves her great-grandchildren, and her appearance is pleasant. She has a welcoming, interesting home and despite her age – ninety-seven – she does not emanate death. My youngest grandson, four-year old Boaz, once said, "Grandma Ruth won't die, she will turn into a caterpillar and then it will turn into a butterfly and fly away."

Do you remember? Your father and his father kissed and your brothers on the lips. The memories seeped into your skin and you can still recall great-grandpa Yehiel's stubble and the softness of great-grandma. She would speak to you in her broken Hebrew, which was peppered with Russian; her clothes had a distinct smell to them,

---

24 Dahlia Ravikovitch "Real Love Isn't What It Seems."

the smell of elsewhere.

Grandpa Shmuel's mother, great-grandma Chaya, lived in a small shack behind her daughter's house. I was scared to go there alone. She was a stooped old woman; she spoke Yiddish and wore a shavis, and I felt uncomfortable in her presence. Appearance was stronger than blood.

Most animals care for their offspring until they are able to survive on their own or spread their wings. Bears, lions and herons do not form relationships with their grandchildren.

My grandchildren are very fortunate to have my mother as their great-grand-mother. The wings of her love somewhat compensate for their loss. Dov's parents, who died at Mauthausen, did not live to see their grandchildren. They have been reduced to a faint flicker of the memorial candle lit on Holocaust Remembrance Day, and the yellowing photograph of an elegant, good-looking couple who once had their whole future ahead of them.

Did David and Rachel Steiger ever give the imaginary me any thought?

Did they picture their son's future love? Did they assume he would return to Carpatho-Russia and attend the University of Prague? Did they imagine welcoming their future grandchildren who would gather raspberries and blueberries at the family's country house near Berezny? Caught in the raging fires that consumed Europe, did anyone even have a thought beyond saving their own life and rescuing the children? Was there any room for a pastoral, peaceful, normal thought?

We met – thirty years after his parents were murdered.

Dov took nothing for granted. Not even having his own children. I am no longer able to share the pleasures and delight in my life with him, and his absence as a grandfather to our grandchildren fills me with great sadness.

Whenever our children were required to trace the "family tree" for their school assignments Dov was minimal in the agenda he volunteered. Names of parents, his own schooling, wars and interests. Nowadays I do it for the grandchildren. Filling in "Grandpa Dov's Side," noting the dry facts. Names, concentration camps, dates and adding background material, WWII , *The Diary of Anne Frank*, the fiction of Aaron Appelfeld, everything was fused with the fertile soil of the farm in Nahalal, the songs of Naomi Shemer, and driven mad by the triumphant blast of the wars of Israel, parents, grandparents and great grandparents,some graveless in marches of death some in graveyards covered with pink cyclamens each winter.

The unfulfilled promise of autumn was cut off by a fierce storm. A genuine storm blanketed Jerusalem in snow, closing off the frozen city, "storm chasers" in the desert drowned in the flood waters and thunderstorms drenched Tel Aviv, covering the city in a thin layer of ice during the freezing nights.

Some of the plants froze overnight. The mandevilla and the pentas leaves dried up and browned and the evergreens shed their foliage. Once again I attempted to tastefully arrange the remains, to accept the fact that my impact is marginal and that there are no answers to my questions, or if there are, my mind cannot grasp them.

Yael Dayan

"I've made a list of questions
to which I no longer expect answers,
since it's either too early for them,
or I won't have time to understand." [25]

Nature has no purpose, no goal or intent. There is no "end to science" and the ability to reach it and realize that we have arrived, is limited.

The cold is restricting; it shrinks my lungs. At home, my hunger for oxygen increases and I need the portable device and the oxygen tube inserted in my nose just to move through the rooms, to go from the bathroom to the bedroom or answer the phone. It's ridiculous, like putting on a nice dress, a pearl necklace, heels and makeup– all so I can walk to the next room and curl up in my feather comforter.

I battle depression tooth and nail. If I can control it, it's not really depression, I tell myself, drying a tear. The tears pool in my eyes but do not roll down my face. For a month I have been adjusting to the new reality now that I have lost my place in public service. It has been two years since I moved to my apartment overlooking the square, the site of my former job, my active life and "public persona" –grandma Pnina's curls, which were white as snow.

I am filled with anxiety at the prospect of silence and at the sight of the blank pages in the notebook.

I am searching for the right recipe for this final chapter, for a sense of certainty regarding what is no longer possible and a taste of fulfillment, even if it is slight, knowing that I have made the most of whatever remains.

Sophisticated formulas have been popping up everywhere. Besides the ones that suggest you trust in god and his mysterious ways, there are also simpler methods that promise incredible results: personal happiness, younger skin and a youthful body, a long life, even great sex included at no extra charge. Any self respecting newspaper, magazine or popular lecture series will present its "ten commandments", which are usually intended for women, and if you follow the rules closely, you will expand your horizons ,revive dead cells, combat cellulites restore your youth, all without giving up the emotional maturity and womanly ripeness gained by age.

The package deal usually includes a healthy breakfast, at least one piece of fruit, leafy green or keratin-rich vegetables, a strict ban on smoking, avoiding alcohol and naturally drugs too, daily exercise ,alone or in company ,moisturizing your face, hands and body and taking age-specific vitamin supplements (some insist on calcium and zinc while others sing the praises of vitamin D, E or both). Limit your intake of sugar and sweets. There are also endless variations on the recommended diet:

No meat, eggs, caffeine, gluten or dairy. Add quinoa, tofu, wheatgrass, garlic skin, turmeric, goat milk and nettle tea and periodically fast, do juice cleansing and perform enemas. Get at least eight hours of sleep, banish everything superficial, pleasurable,

---

25 Wislawa Szymborska "List" Translated by Stanislaw Baranczak and Clare Cavanagh.

loud, tasty and satisfying.

I was never tempted to try any of it, and if I did – it was on doctor's orders and only for a short while. I am jealous of women whose skin doesn't reveal their age and don't have wrinkles on their necks or veins on their legs. Women who are blessed with a slow agin gprocess, and even those that sought the help of a competent plastic surgeon or used collagen rebuilding cells and wrinkle filling injections.

I find it hard to be jealous of my mother. Compared to her, I will always fall short and I accept this fact without resentment. There is no chance that in twenty, ten or even five years, I will have her aura of goodness, her joie de vivre, or will be able to match the interest that she takes in people and her tendency to always see the best in them, particularly when they are members of our rapidly expanding family. I have no doubt that a lenient interpretation of reality and downplaying damage have a positive impact on longevity. Her sources of energy are of mythological enormity.

My ninety-seven-year-old mother does not have a list of do's and don'ts for a long and rewarding life. Grandma Rachel didn't have one either; she favored moderation over restriction. To this day, my mother smokes in moderation and she is no stranger to the pleasures of a glass of a single malt whiskey or a fine cognac.

They didn't count their wrinkles or the age spots on their hands, neither believed in God and both were equally harsh on people in terms of moral culpability and the responsibility they must take for their actions. My mother is more forgiving, she does not bear grudges. Takes pleasure in the little things. For better or for worse, there is absolutely no chance that I inherited her gene-pool in its entirety.

My mother has the need to nurse, caress, comfort and hold her children's hands.

My younger brother was willing to be nurtured and coddled, due both to his character and the circumstances he created; he found a way to attach himself to the umbilical cord, and he was the center of her life. He was the focus of her love and concern, the reason for her existence and he dominated her days, a source of pride and despair.

My other brother visited mother often, but took care to limit any intrusion on his privacy. He was content with her love, her concern for his health and her soup.

"Udi came by and had some soup," is her daily mantra, and I listen with the patience that my children do not show me, grateful to have the opportunity to rectify past transgressions. Lovingly, we laugh at it all; the weariness of life, her tireless activity, her innate inability to say no, and the palpable end facing us both. And we wonder who will make soup for Udi when the other is gone keeping the culinary diversity of Chicken, Tomato and Borscht.

Both of us miss her mother, Grandma Rachel, who lived a full life and died at 97 when she felt it was void of meaning ,repetitious and a burden to others.

My seventy-fifth birthday has arrived, it is also the eleventh anniversary of Dov's death and my mother's ninety-seventh birthday. Winter events. Yet this year the balance in my life has been upset.

Closely examining my desolation, I find no good tidings and nothing positive about marking my age. I am envious of everyone who is different from me, who doesn't face physical disabilities and ages with refinement and grace.

I asked a neurosurgeon friend to give me an MRI image of my brain as a birthday present. Perhaps a disc with the genome and an MRI of my brain will be able to decipher what lies hidden inside me. Maybe I could even be cloned, if anyone would want to do that. Perhaps, unbeknownst to ourselves, we are already perfect clones; a fantasy that need not be proved or justified, a non-violent fairy tale

With my mother in the final stretch of her centennial, I find it hard to begin a new count and enter my seventy-fifth year.

The changing seasons have passed over winter, delivering me a harsh blow. A week-long freezing storm and a cold front destroyed the plants and brought the unfulfilled promise of rain. After weeks of expectation, the sky and the sea were still hazy and both my body and the clouds were dry and restless, until it became clear that winter would not return and was gone for good. I felt the premature hot eastern winds blow and my throat was parched with thirst.

The subsequent blossoming of the plants was unexpected and struck with violent intensity, disrupting the established order and confusing the senses. The bulbs, which had been counting on the chilly nights of winter, were now preceded by the sweet peas that bloomed abundantly in every possible color and genetic variation. Instantly, the balcony was covered in a dizzyingly yellow-orange flash of nasturtiums. The bees and insects pounced on them, buzzing amongst the butterflies and honey-suckers, intent on the nectar that flowed freely, circling the flowers like drug addicts. The wild pigeons and the parakeets mated early too, perching on the windowsills and rooftops, and the quiet hot air remained still, relinquishing its desire for wind and moisture.

I am like a dry stream that lost its path, as the winter dropped out of my life. I have paused, and am unable to flow in the thick air. The starlings are still here and the swallows arrived early, the green leaves have awakened before hibernation had a chance to descend upon them and the margosa tree is early to bloom, dotting the sidewalk light purple.

I have nowhere else to take my fragmentary reckoning.

The High Holidays made way for a partial, incomplete autumn and an absent life-sustaining winter . It is spring now and the air is already heavy with the promise of summer.

We meet beside Dov's grave in the heat of the day.

There are numerous graves surrounding his preventing us from getting close.

Eleven years ago Rachel Corrie was killed by an IDF bulldozer as she tried to stop the destruction of a house in Rafah, and two days ago in the village of Dir El Assal, Youssef A-Swamrah, a young boy, was shot and killed as he passed through a hole in the fence in order to pick a'kub, edible sunflower plants, from his family's plot in South Mt. Hebron. What has changed in over a decade? Between the deaths of Rachel and Youssef, between Rafah that we evacuated and the settlement of Itzhar, which crushes hope with its poisonous bite. And how have I changed in the decade and a year since Dov's death as I now stand beside his grave with my children, my mother, a handful of my friends and his colleagues, all gathered together, smiling memories.

Transitions

I cannot put the sequence of events in their proper order. It seems that the length, or the limit, of my life does not correspond with the breadth of my longing. I will proceed with care, fending off commotion and trying not to lose my footing by expecting what is unlikely to happen.

Rabbi Nachman said: "A man can revive the dead by going to and fro within his home." I wonder if the saying itself, the very act of movement, could extend life.

On this end, in this house, at this age, there is no room to stretch out. Any extension of the hand meets with locked rooms.

I will likely hover in place above this narrow circle, embracing the fortunes within it, moving farther away and getting smaller until the only thing that remains of me and of them are the flowing, fading words and the blessing of silence.

Chapter 14

May 2014. The death of my younger brother Assi.
To end with a scream or a sigh?

On a Thursday morning in the beginning of a summery spring, my younger brother Assi died. He was seven years– and entire generation – my junior.

Assi wrote his life and he wrote his death; he eulogized himself and rose to reclaim the crown time and again. A phoenix , the handsomest of young men, captivating and intelligent, a man who did not know when to stop. Assi lived on the edge; he didn't want to die, but his will to live wasn't strong enough to accurately gage the distance between "on the brink of disaster" and disaster itself.

We led parallel lives, grew apart, and also overlapped and changed trajectories.

He was always my little brother and I his elder sister. Many times I found myself helpless, unable to remove the obstacles that were blocking his path, obstacles that he piled up himself. He attracted and repelled, loved and loathed, created and destroyed, and no one could stand in his way.

To our mother he was always the baby, and in time, during his final years, he became the sick child. A source of anxiety, preoccupation, care and tears. He had the power to either crush her or bring her back to life, and he indulged himself, using her and hurting along with her. They strode hand-in-hand like an ill-fated pair, falling and rising up again. She was upright and erect; he was stooped and slouched over. An incurable mother and son, a beautiful lioness noble in her old age and her wounded cub, who left behind a trail of bloody prints as if he were sprinkling golden crumbs. Her path was of infinite motherhood, he took the path of finality.

Assi was buried in Shimron, the cemetary of Nahalal, our birth village, in a new plot on the slope of the hill situated at the foot of our father's and our paternal grand-parents' graves, looking out on the valley, with the adjacent burial plot reserved for our mother.

Perhaps Assi's wish to be buried by his father's side, "near his family members" was his way of reconciliation, as if to say that only death could make peace between them.

Some of the drawers can now be opened in the locked room. Assi guarded and nurtured a spite towards our father which I considered unfounded. I accepted the prevailing myths in the family about an estranged father, a legendary mother, a beloved favorite daughter, and the various deprivations and deficiencies that we experienced in childhood. If they were false and deceitful, at times intentionally harmful,there seemed no point in revealing it. We all have our different versions, and even if I did not acknowledge someone else's story, I didn't dare harm the fragile life that fed upon it. When a myth turns into a comforting shelter padding its subject in layers of fabricated love or hate, perhaps it is forbidden to tamper with it. I am afraid of shattering something that is not in my power to restore. Not within myself either.

We were different in that respect.

Your brother did not feel unloved, but he was hurt by your father's disdain for the quality of his poetry – which either existed or did not. You cannot know, and perhaps he too forgot the truth, as the fabric of his days began unraveling at the seams, and he did not discern the rifts, nor did he patch them up. All that remained was a blinding misleading glitter.

There were also long intervals when he chose to disconnect , absences which raised anxiety and suggested he was sliding down a slope, not wanting to be stopped or saved.

You never knew whether Assi would return in order to reconnect and what kind of weapon he would be bearing and who would be blamed with what, and if the guilty party would forever be your father, like an angry god from whose forehead he was borne and was never accepted into the paternal bosom, or if the victim would be your mother, or you, or your brother Udi.

You were all targets for slanderous and nullifying attacks that ended with Assi apologizing, regretting what had been written, and offering his poems as compensation. There were moving poems for your mother on her birthdays:

> "The days of our bad old age are still to come
> We will stumble toward you, who is forever youthful"

As he wrote on her ninety-second birthday, and a year later, when your mother turned ninety-three, he wrote:

> "And I who settled in your lap
> bless you with all long life
> for my own is slowly failing."

You harbored the disconcerting, shameful hope that she would outlive him, because only your mother could sustain him with love and patience, could accept his loss of direction along with the sparks of wisdom that he uttered and his tormented brain and physical suffering.

His four children, the eldest is like a sister to your daughter. His wives, ex-wives, his loves, granddaughters and grandson, his works of art and his awards, a life's work decorating the tumultuous path that he tread upon, none of them were a match to his demons, his fearful hallucinations and violent outbursts. Only your mother could absorb it all. She contained it, paid a heavy price and finally outlived him, and his untimely death was better than his life without your mother.

I loved my little brother, I had compassion for the distorted life he led. I feared his violence when he lost control. My understanding was not sufficient to accept or forgive his inability to cope during the years when it was still possible, his refusal to take responsibility, and his constant, manipulative demands .

He wanted to live on his own terms, in the chaos that he had created, with the echo of his cinematic genius and his perforated health- brain, heart, lungs, liver – lamenting himself, defying death and clinging to mother.

Assi translated Dylan Thomas into Hebrew, "Do Not Go Gentle Into That Good Night" and "And Death Shall Have No Dominion" and died with the thought that he managed to survive another night of revelry, of wild, infinitely unsatisfying addiction.

My brother loved me and often avoided me, fearing my judgment and criticism. He knew I could see through him and it added discomfort to his unstable love.

And so, another shiva. Only something completely predictable could be so sudden. It was entirely expected. Every year, every month, every stint in the hospital, each time the ambulance was called, every suicide attempt, every overdose, every bizarre "final" conversation that he initiated, each farewell letter and parting poem– until we got accustomed to it. We got used to his life and not to the suddenness of his death.

People, hundreds of people, come and go from his shiva and do not ask questions. Two of his children have been orphaned this year, with the loss of their mother, Aharona, just months earlier.

The media showered him with accolades and laurels that would have been a great source of pleasure to him when he was alive, family, friends and acquaintances turned into admirers, mother was comforted by four generations of friends, their children and grandchildren and a handful of well- wishers who came in order to people-watch in the crowded apartment, sampling the pastries and trying to guess the identities of the famous people who made their way in and out.

I am grateful for my bright and beloved aunt Reuma, who shares the love and care for my mother, her only sister, and helps her through these difficult days.

Thousands of papers have piled up in Assi's apartment– printed pages, bits and pieces of scripts, stories, poems, scraps of synopses, old scripts, hundreds of dusty books, computer drawings covering the walls from floor to ceiling, newspaper clippings, photographs of Kafka, Einstein, Freud, his children, actresses– that he had collected,cut out and pasted on the wall with a rigid, fixed and permanent obsession.

A kind of wailing wall, a testament to a form of mental activity that bounced between the rational, memory and the imagination and the realms of hallucination, traversing the peaks of humor and the depths of anxiety and despair.

In a poem he wrote on my seventieth birthday, my brother beckons to me from

Yael Dayan

"underneath the cypress trees at Shimron" but my place will not be there. You alone are embraced, darling boy, mama's baby, overlooking Nahalal, amongst your family and without your siblings. You chose to "come home" to the house that you never inhabited and in which you found comfort, unwinding from your turbulent life. You raged and you enraged with glorious gusts, and now it ends.

A thank you note was sent to all who came to offer consolation. Mother's house contained remains of the cookies, photographs and unworn clothes, the meaningless utterances when words ran out, the dry eyes when people were around, the mother whose son has orphaned her.

Udi and I can never fill Assi's empty space and she cries her heart out every night, her life now marred by a fatigue that has no remedy.

In Nahalal, wilting wreaths cover a mound of volcanic earth and soon there will be a heavy marble tombstone bearing the inscription:

Assi Dayan
Son of Ruth and Moshe 1945-2014

I resume my daily routine and the little that remains.

I bid farewell to the white page and close the gap between what is brimming within me and the act of documenting it. I bid farewell to the preoccupation with bodily anguish and my health in the last years. I must try to make the most of the avenues that are not obstructed, to tread along the paths that time has treated kindly or has equipped with warning signs, keeping them free of banality and humiliation.

I am not closing off a life but rather sealing a random report of what was important, like adding a leavening agent to a mixture that hasn't been sifted carefully enough. I have little need for provisions on the short journey remaining.

My mother, soon one hundred years-old, may she live long, has folded into her grief. She is still active and accessible, but her eyes are focused on the good times in the past, and she oscillates between them and the injustices of the present. She has long since reconciled her inability to shape the face of the future.

My children, as part of the course of nature, have flattened the umbilical cord into an invisible thin thread, which at times only goes one-way, is unavailable or is based on the demands of daily life and its cultivation necessitates caution.

I love and cherish the close friends that remain. Those who haven't been erased from the book of the living and the address book that I update every year, or haven't travelled across oceans and never pop up in tweets or on Facebook, or haven't been carried off by asinine thoughts with which I can find no common ground.

Younger friends have joined them, they look forward to a future that differs from my own and do not stand on the finishing line, rummaging through the leftovers. With them I search for answers to my musings, affirmations for hopes and fears and solutions to the gap between technological and scientific progress and the nature of man, his follies and his numbered days on this earth.

And the rest of the path is brightened by my love of the grandchildren. The innocent joy, the minor disappointments and surprises, dreams fulfilled and fears overcome, the laughter and tears that change in a flash, leaving the sky above me glowing with rainbows and blossoming with joy.

And what about settling accounts? All the accounts that have yet to be settled between generations. The promises we made to our children, the promises that were made to us by our parents, debts that have been stained by our sweat, tears and toil, and even though they haven't been paid off in full, the intent was there.

Now they are gone, or it is too late to redeem them, or they have aged and lost their value. The score to settle with my father, which wasn't my own undertaking, has been forgotten and forgiven. The debts of leaders – the promises in which I invested fantasies and much work and some delusions, which have been shattered instantaneously and transformed into a bitter and humiliating swamp, even those have dried out and been pushed aside. Scores I haven't settled, disappointments I caused, expectations I did not fulfill as I left someone waiting in vain by the side of the road or near the summit which he never would've been able to reach without me.

My escapes from an obsessive suitor, an unwanted pregnancy, from the justified rage at me, from reproach and criticism that caused me discomfort.

Accounts have been settled. I have forgiven, and whoever has not forgiven me can come and get their apology, for I am neither running away nor attempting to hide.

And what about the memories? The very small ones that weren't written down, the minute ones that are trivial to a stranger but seize my heart and refuse to simply slip away. The rustle of a floor-length dress at a formal reception, the intoxicating scent of a lover's cologne. Childhood memories of the fear that gripped me at night when I walked to the outhouse in Nahalal, my first bicycle, secondhand, without a "top tube" on the frame, the sacs of carobs used for chicken feed, and how we would puncture them and eat the black dry fruit that caused a rough chill on our teeth. Jericho in bloom and the pomelos and the crates of citrus fruit by the side of the road, the mango juice stands lining the Alexandria- Cairo road, an airport goodbye in Africa, parting from a friend who was killed several days later, having blinis with caviar at a restaurant in Rio, bathing in a tub heated by an open fire at a hotel in Kathmandu, riding the night train from Moscow to St. Petersburg with a friend, and the small bottle of vodka and sandwiches we shared behind the bolted door, frightened by the tales of thieves who drugged passengers on the train. All the little memories that have sifted through the sieve, dotting my life with butterfly-like colors.

> "And the missing elements and the added silences. And you, what do you do in the remainder of your life between the memories and the medications." [26]

---

26 Haim Gouri, "Eyval".

Yael Dayan

And what of all this beauty? The beauty that is not taken for granted, which cannot always be perceived and merely passes by, for life is always too short to contain it. The beauty of alluring poetry, bewitching music and magical artwork. The beauty of the germinating seed and the birth of all creatures and the dread of sunset and the delight of sunrise. The changing of the seasons, the galloping progress of science, the liberties of men and women. The beauty of my poor, captivating land, weighed down with history and a slave to its imaginary messianic destiny. Torn apart right down to its marrow and hopelessly loved from the awe-inspiring desert in the south to the playful babble of the brooks and the songbirds in the north.

And all of the beauty, abundance and opportunities, the wealth and the bleeding schisms are hidden under a black cloud of power-hungry gamblers who lead the country with the insane vision of occupation, annexation, seizing the land of others and turning all of the goodness into a fortress, an arsenal. Living by the sword. A "community of victims" whose dead determines the course of the crusade that the living are forced to follow.

And on the opposite side, similarly, Muslim extremists are reviving the Caliphate from Iraq, Syria, Lebanon and Jordan, paving it with corpses in a frenzy of crazed desire that may reach our borders. We could all be swept up into a religious war, if we don't have the foresight to join those not guided by God or Allah, and put an end to our appetite.

I part from the pages but not from my passionate commitments. Submerged in a pool of sadness and missed opportunities, I know that there is no other solution but that of Two States. Jerusalem will have to be repartitioned and we will save our disintegrating democracy from distortion and abuse in the name of God. I trust that there will be an end to the corruption, folly, injustice and violence and I want to be there when it happens. And if not right there, I'd like to stand a hairsbreadth away and be able to witness the burgeoning hope.

"Salaam is the apology of the might to the one / with weaker weapons and stronger range."

Our range is short sighted.

"Salaam is the sword breaking in front of natural / beauty, when dew smelts the iron." [27]

And the dew, natural, patient and consistent, can and will hold its ground against the aloof iron entity we have become and overpower it.

And what else remains? Scarves of silk and wool, tulle and soft cotton, scarves in a multitude of patterns and all the colors of the rainbow. Beads of amber, glass, silver and gold, designed for prayer, ornament, beauty or luck, the wood and turquoise necklaces, several with missing clasps, scattered, still bearing the scents of the market stalls of Tunisia and Istanbul.

---

27 Mahmoud Darwish, *State of Siege.*

Transitions

The fears remain, those that have been fastened with rusty locks and those that are out in the open, printed on the pages of the newspapers. New galaxies have been discovered, artificial intelligence threatens the boundaries that we have learned to respect.

Millions of laboratory stem cells differentiate into tissue and organ, and are readily utilized for salutary remedies and the frightening prospect of unnatural cloning. We have grown accustomed to the "natural" and mutations as part of its course. The primal fear of the unknown has shrunk in size as new avenues have opened up to scientists, transforming the mysterious into the comprehensible, harnessing computer languages to the process of protein folding and promising to decipher the secrets of the mind and heal its ills. I am impatient now and I want all of the answers; for diseases, for that which is deficient, lacking or absent, or flawed. I am in a hurry, the road ahead is misty and I find it hard to take an interest in what will happen thousands or millions of years from now.

Global warming, melting glaciers causing flooded cities, a cure for autoimmune deficiencies, genetically matching medicines to malignancies, robotics for all and in all things, populating Mars, eradicating violence, telepathic communication that can bypass electronics, the liberation of the computer from its inventors and programmers, three-dimensional printing of organs for transplant purposes, creating a new kind of "natural"... What will I still manage to witness in my lifetime? In the lifetime of my children and grandchildren?

I am aware of the brevity of my life and am ready to relinquish satisfying desires for a state of tranquil fatigue. To lovingly put on the "cloak of forgetfulness" and the muteness of twilight, to be given the blessing:

> "Happy are they who sow and do not reap
> for they shall wander afar." [28]

I am prepared to sow without the promise of harvest but I am unwilling to go into darkness and I can see the lights yonder, from afar.

---

28 Avraham Ben Yitzhak "Happy Are They Who Sow".

Excerpts in the book appear in the following works:

Avraham Ben-Yitzhak, "Happy Are They Who Sow" from Collected Poems, Translated by Peter Cole, Ibis Publishing, 2003.

Assi Dayan, two poems from But Love, Even Hoshen Publishing, 2012 (Hebrew).

Dahlia Ravikovitch, "Hovering at a Low Altitude" and "True Love Isn't What It Seems", from Hovering at a Low Altitude: The Collected Poetry of Dahlia Ravikovitch, Translated by Chana Bloch and Chana Kronfeld, W.W. Norton and Co., 2011.

Wislawa Szymborska, "List" from Chwila: Moment, Translated by Clare Cavanagh and Stanislaw Baranczak, Wydawnictwo Znak Publishers, 2003.

Haim Gouri, "Eyval", from Eyval, Hakibbutz Hameuchad Publishing, 2009 (Hebrew).

Josef Brodsky, "A Part of Speech" from Collected Poems in English, 1972-1999, Farrar Straus and Giroux, 2000.

Yael Dayan, My Father, His Daughter, Farrar Straus & Giroux, 1985. Yael Dayan, Death Had Two Sons, McGraw-Hill, 1967.
Rebbe Nachman of Breslov Likutey Moharan Book 1

Mahmoud Darwish, State of Siege, Translated by Munir Akash, Syracuse University Press, 2010.

Czeslaw Milosz, "Prescription" from New And Collected Poems: 1931-2001, Translated by Robert Haas, Ecco, 2003.

Karel Capek The Gardener's Year, Modern Library, 2002.

C.P. Cavafy, Collected Poems. Translated by Edmund Keeley and Philip Sherrard. Edited by George Savidis. Revised Edition. Princeton University Press, 1992.

Ra'hel Bluwstein, Flowers of Perhaps: Selected Poems of Ra'hel, Translated by Robert Friend, The Menard Press, 1994.

T.S. Elliot "The Hollow Men", Selected Poems, Mariner Books, 1967.

Acknowledgements

The wisdom, encouragement, skill and love of a few friends enabled the writing of this Memoir. I thank Orly Castel-Bloom, Savion Liebrecht, Professor David Harel, Mooky Dagan and Dr. Giddon Ticotski. My gratitude also goes to my Mosaic editor Mike Walsh, to Karen And Barry Fierst, Susan(Yael) Mesinai and Lilly Rivlin who patiently and wisely bridged gaps - chronological, mental and linguistic-between the Hebrew and the English readers.